KV-060-707

NEW PATHFINDER

Making the case for languages at Key Stage 4

LINDA PARKER &
TERESA TINSLEY

5

Association for Language Learning

CiLT The National Centre for Languages

First published 2005
by CILT, the National Centre for Languages
20 Bedfordbury
London
WC2N 4LB

Copyright © CILT, the National Centre for Languages 2005

ISBN 1 904243 45 2

A catalogue record for this book is available from the British Library

All rights reserved. No part of this publication may be reproduced, stored in a retrieval system, or transmitted by any other means, electronic, mechanical, photocopying, recording or otherwise without prior permission in writing from CILT, the National Centre for Languages or under licence from the Copyright Licensing Agency Limited, of 90 Tottenham Court Road, London W1T 4LP.

The right of Linda Parker and Teresa Tinsley to be identified as authors of this work has been asserted by them in accordance with the Copyright, Designs and Patents Act, 1988.

Printed in Great Britain by Hobbs the Printers Ltd

CILT Publications may be ordered from **Central Books**, 99 Wallis Rd, London E9 5LN. Tel: 0845 458 9910. Fax: 0845 458 9912.

contents

Acknowledgements

This book is dedicated to the late Peter Boaks whose conviction that languages improve the lives of young people inspired his work and ours.

The authors are indebted to Peter for his encouragement and guidance with this project, to Henriette Harnisch for her support, inspiration and contributions, to Ruth Bailey for her advice and comments on the manuscript, and to Barry Jones for his excellent Foreword. Teresa would also like to thank staff, Management and fellow Governors at Hampstead School for the insights they provided.

Foreword

At a time when foreign language teaching and learning is the subject of both positive and negative scrutiny, this book is timely and much needed. Its carefully reasoned arguments are not just confirmation of what most modern language teachers strongly believe, but make the case explicitly and persuasively for a range of audiences including Governors, parents and their local communities, other subject teachers and the learners themselves. Its approach is informed, carefully researched and presented in a way which can be directly transmitted to those whom it seeks to inform and persuade.

Language teachers will be pleased – and reassured – to see their subject rightly considered as not only making a valuable contribution to the social and intellectual development of learners, but also as a practical skill. They will also find themselves armed with an array of up-to-date, broadly based arguments which focus on cultural as well as linguistic gains which accrue from learning and using another language – an aspect not always fully appreciated, particularly by policy- and decision-makers who may not be linguists or who may themselves have had negative language-learning experiences. The range and scope of this exploration is such that a strong case can be made efficiently by tailoring its content to fit a particular context.

The realistic approach adopted in this book does not ignore problems and challenges, but describes and analyses them fully. This feature will greatly assist anyone trying to predict, and subsequently answer, potential questions posed by those whom they are seeking to convince. It makes a useful distinction between what it sees as the 'old mindset' and a 'new vision', an important analysis which shows how much attitudes to language learning have changed in recent times, especially in other parts of Europe. It also uses to enhance its case neat ways of meeting the concerns of Headteachers and others, and showing how language learning can support their efforts rather than be seen as an obstacle.

Achieving status within the school and within the wider community is explored with some imaginative examples and creative thinking. For even the best departments, the wealth of ideas for integrating what they do with the work of others in the school, at both practical and policy levels, makes inspiring reading. To be able to change attitudes – always problematic – looks feasible not just from the suggestions in the text, but also from nicely chosen case studies. The involvement of parents, and taking full advantage of what the local community can offer, is also explored so convincingly that readers will be motivated to experiment with or adapt existing practice.

Changing the mindset of learners in school is perhaps the greatest challenge which the book tackles. In addition to better and more accurate guidance regarding the usefulness and value of language learning, the list of promotional techniques and general ploys to encourage and persuade our 'customers' is practical and constructive. As the book illustrates, learners need short-term, even immediate goals, as well as a better understanding in the longer term of what language learning can offer. This section also illustrates convincingly that speaking to pupils and involving them in decisions about their language learning is not only revealing, but can help us tailor and adapt classroom practice to what motivates and engages learners.

The final part of the last chapter 'answering pupils' questions' is key. If modern language teachers in their departments have discussed and found – albeit provisional – answers to these common statements about language learning, the more convincing their responses will be. Better still – and if possible during professional activities organised for example by the Association for Language Learning and CILT – we can develop a common approach by discussing with other professionals how to enhance the status of language learning, not just among our pupils but within the school and wider community. If we want to know where to start, we have no further to look than the chapters of this excellent book.

Barry Jones, President 2004–2005
Association for Language Learning

Introduction

The statutory position regarding languages in Key Stage 4 has changed, but the conviction of many language teachers that languages are of benefit to most, if not all, pupils has not. Some teachers, while perhaps relieved that they will no longer have to teach large classes of unwilling teenagers, are worried about the erosion of the status of their subject within the school and may be concerned that many able linguists, too, are now able to opt out of language study.

Whose job is it to solve the crisis in languages post-14? Surely the Government could solve our problems at a stroke by giving languages back its compulsory status? The Government does indeed wield a lot of influence and it is to be hoped that it will take action in the context of the *14–19 Education and Skills White Paper* (2005) to bolster the statutory position of languages, but this book takes as its starting point that the role of the language teacher is vital, too. Teachers are not mere pawns in the game, but can be active players in making the case for their subject, whatever the policy context. Unlike the Government, they have direct day-to-day contact with pupils, colleagues, Senior Management and wider communities, and can play a huge role in helping them to think positively about languages. If they do this job well, students will be more motivated and will achieve better results, whether or not languages are a compulsory component in the curriculum. There is already a wealth of good practice, but Heads of Department may feel isolated, lacking the tools or the time to push forward this sort of work, and under the impression that whatever they do, they may be reinventing the wheel. *Making the case for languages at Key Stage 4* is written to address these needs.

We are in a new situation now and this provides us with an opportunity – and of course a need – to make a strong case for language learning as never before, in order to compete with other subjects for a place in the curriculum, but also to communicate what we know to be right. The debate surrounding the entitlement curriculum makes much of the issue of pupil choice, casting languages in the role of an unpopular subject with teenagers (although there is nothing to suggest that subjects like Maths or Science would not be equally 'unpopular' if made optional). We will take a closer look at pupil attitudes and motivation in Chapter 4 of this book, and present ideas and arguments likely to be effective in convincing pupils that it is worth persevering with languages.

However, as a report into the position of languages in the North East points out, 'the numbers continuing with a language at Key Stage 4 are determined primarily by school policy' (Harrison 2004). The Government has effectively delegated responsibility for languages post-14 to schools and Headteachers will need up-to-date information and an understanding of the issues to make sound decisions which will affect the futures of over half a million young people annually. The 2005 OFSTED report on implementing Modern Foreign Languages entitlement in Key Stage 4 drew attention to the importance, for languages to flourish, of strong SMT support for languages and a commitment to preventing MFL from becoming an elitist subject.

We therefore devote Chapter 1 to making the case for languages to Senior Management and School Governors. Chapters 3 and 4 look at two other groups of stakeholders who are important in creating a language-friendly environment: parents and the community, and other subject teachers within the school. This book thus presents a four-pronged approach to informing, convincing and ultimately changing the mindset of these four groups who have the power to make or break the future of languages within a school.

The introduction will now focus on answering some general questions about where we are today with languages, how we got here – and what the future holds.

What is the current statutory position regarding languages in Key Stage 4?

From September 2004, Modern Foreign Languages are one of four 'statutory entitlement areas' at Key Stage 4. This means that every school must provide the opportunity for all students to take a course in languages in KS4, as well as in the other entitlement areas of Arts, Humanities and Design and Technology. The course must lead to a qualification approved under Section 96 of the Learning and Skills Act 2000.

This means that schools should not:

- set up option systems in a way which forces students to choose between these entitlement areas, since all students should be able to take a course in each of the entitlement areas, if they choose to do so (i.e. students should not have to choose between a language and an artistic subject);

- set up option systems which debar certain groups of students from choosing a language (i.e. guiding certain groups of students into 'vocational' options which are timetabled against languages);

- cut options on the basis of low numbers, if this means that students who have expressed a wish to study a language are not able to do so.

Full details of the statutory requirements for languages at KS4 are given in the QCA booklet *Modern Foreign Languages in the Key Stage 4 curriculum*, available at **www.qca.org.uk/13680.html**.

What level of provision does OFSTED regard as acceptable?

According to Her Majesty's Chief Inspector of Schools, David Bell, '… Modern Foreign Languages is an important part of the curriculum for pupils from all backgrounds. Schools, teachers and parents must now work to ensure that pupils recognise the benefits of learning a foreign language and make sure that young people have the opportunity and desire to continue studying a Modern Foreign Language at Key Stage 4 and beyond'.

OFSTED's report, *Implementing Modern Foreign Languages entitlement in Key Stage 4* (2005a) made four recommendations for schools to consider:

- how to ensure that a wider vocational offer in other subjects at Key Stage 4 does not preclude students from continuing with MFL;

- how to improve students' use of ICT in their MFL learning and increase their access to recent authentic materials;

- how to offer a wider range of MFL courses and accreditation at Key Stage 4, including vocational qualifications;

- ways to enable larger numbers of students to study two languages in Key Stage 4.

How have we got where we are today? (Have 'languages for all' and GCSE been a failure?)

As former Director of CILT, Alan Moys, has pointed out (1996), languages was the subject most affected by the move to comprehensive education, with most schools setting themselves the target for the first time of teaching a language for all pupils from 11 to 14. Although most pupils then dropped the subject, there was a steady increase in the numbers taking GCE and CSE exams, from 225,848 in 1965 to 415,888 in 1985. Numbers continued to rise with the introduction of GCSE in 1986 and from 1990 onwards as the National Curriculum was phased in, with languages becoming a compulsory subject from 11 to 16. By 1995 the numbers being entered for GCSE in a language reached 547,224 and well over half a million students a year have taken a GCSE in a language from then on.

Compared with the figures for History (230,688 in 2004), Design and Technology (437,403) and Media Studies (39,820), this hardly looks like a failure. Only Maths, English and Science have higher numbers of candidates and there are more students taking a GCSE in German than in either Drama or ICT, more taking French than either History or Geography, and more taking Spanish than Media Studies.

GCSE entry figures for 2005

Language	Candidate numbers
French	272,140
German	105,288
Spanish	62,456
Welsh L2	9,800
Urdu	6,334
Italian	5,492
Welsh	5,098
Chinese	3,091
Irish	2,507
Arabic	2,183
Bengali	1,865

Russian	1,736
Panjabi	1,341
Turkish	1,337
Japanese	1,120
Gujarati	1,080
Portuguese	1,028
Modern Greek	604
Modern Hebrew	442
Persian	441
Polish	405
Dutch	380
Total MFL	*486,168*
All subject entries	*5,736,505*
% MFL of total entries	*8.5%*

The 'failure' – and this is probably not in fact a direct result of the 'languages for all' policy – is in the low take-up rates post-16. Peter Boaks (1998: 34–43) referred to the 'crisis' in languages post-16 in 1998, 'at this point nine out of ten young people discontinue study of a language. This represents a serious missed opportunity for young people'.

The poor progression rates to AS and A2 have been attributed to unsatisfactory experiences of language learning at GCSE and in the National Curriculum in general. In the words of Gary Chambers (2001), 'the National Curriculum has failed to provide pupils with a learning experience which interests and excites them'. The 'treadmill of topics' and poor cultural content of courses has also been identified as a contributory stumbling block. As one contributor to the Lingu@NET forum put it, as this book was in preparation, 'this over-dwelling on topics, both at GCSE and A level, seems to be turning language learning into some form of death-by-boring-content syndrome'.

The debate about what the content of secondary school language courses should be, and how far they are determined by exam specifications, is not one we can do justice to in this book. Nor do we intend to discuss teaching approaches or issues relating to pedagogy which may have an effect on students' decisions to continue with a language. There is extensive and highly recommended literature on these available through the CILT Library and ALL journals.

What is the state of provision in schools across the country?

In 2002, the Government published its Green Paper on the 14–19 curriculum, *Extending opportunity, raising standards* (DfES 2002a), which encouraged schools to diversify provision in Key Stage 4. Releasing students from the obligation to study a language has been seen by many as a means of freeing up the curriculum for other subjects and, as the figures below show, this has happened more quickly and more extensively than perhaps the Government had foreseen. Since 2002, CILT and the Association for Language Learning (ALL) have been organising annual surveys to track the changing position of languages in Key Stage 4. The results of these surveys so far paint a disturbing picture:

- in 2002, 25% of schools had taken the decision to make languages optional in KS4;
- in 2003, 43% of schools had done so;
- in 2004, between 65% and 70% of schools had made languages optional;
- by 2005 this had risen to 75%.

The entitlement curriculum for KS4 finally became official in September 2004. The fact that schools were already 'jumping the gun' in introducing a greater element of choice, can be seen as evidence of eagerness on the part of schools to take on the challenge of making the post-14 curriculum more relevant and motivating for students and of making sure that students at the lower end of ability, in particular, should get the best possible results – with league tables never far from consideration. In many ways, these are exactly the challenges identified for languages. There is absolutely no conflict between the desire for a relevant and motivating curriculum, and studying a language. On the other hand, perhaps the terms 'relevant and motivating' are being used as shorthand for something else. As we pointed out in the 2004 *Language Trends* survey (CILT/ALL/ISMLA 2004), languages are unfortunately being cast in opposition to the 'vocational' choices which are being opened up to students. Teachers who replied to the 2004 survey criticised, in particular, the way subjects like Leisure and Tourism and Business Studies, in which languages are supremely relevant, are being offered as alternatives to languages. The perception that languages are neither a basic part of education, nor practical and relevant for all belies a serious misapprehension about the nature and purposes of language teaching at school level. In making the case for languages, we will need to address this misapprehension, showing how learning languages can provide both a practical skill and a significant contribution to intellectual and social development, as well as adapting our offer of courses and qualifications to suit the needs of a wide range of students. In this way, we can ensure that numbers are high and at the same time address some long-standing weaknesses in our subject.

How does the current policy sit with the National Languages Strategy?

In December 2002, the Government published its National Languages Strategy, *Languages for all, languages for life*, which brought the focus on languages in the curriculum into Key Stages 2 and 3. The rationale for this was that pupils who enjoyed a positive experience of language learning earlier on would be more motivated to continue studying one in Key Stage 4 and beyond; however this 'long-burn' policy was harshly criticised as offering nothing to the current generation of secondary school students who are increasingly dropping languages, without having had the benefit of an earlier start. The challenges for secondary schools are now threefold:

- how to ensure smooth transition for Year 7 pupils, an increasing number of whom will be arriving with some prior experience of language learning (CILT's Young Pathfinder 13: *Mind the gap!* (Bevis and Gregory 2005) should be a useful support here);

- how to ensure excellent language provision in KS3, in a context where there is a risk of the subject appearing to have been 'devalued';

- how to diversify language provision in KS4 (and beyond), offering courses which match the needs of the full range of learners, including both vocational and academic options.

The Languages Ladder, or National Recognition Scheme for languages, was one of the three main objectives of the National Languages Strategy and was launched in 2005. The Ladder offers some exciting opportunities for languages in KS4.

It allows pupils to be assessed separately in the four skills, as and when they are ready. The system of grades (likened to music grades) means that pupils will potentially be able to give up languages for a year or two, then pick them up at the next level. It will be hugely beneficial for pupils who do give up after KS3, allowing them to take something away from three years' study. It could also open the way for innovative timetabling of short intensive courses which take students quickly to the next level (in one or more skills). This could be highly motivating. The short steps between the grades should allow pupils to feel they are getting somewhere quickly and measure their progress.

The Languages Ladder – and the qualifications linked to it provided by Asset Languages which qualify for performance points – will be crucial in helping us build a more flexible offer to cater for different levels and different languages at different points in a student's career. The fit with 'personalised' education and the potential to draw community languages into the mainstream offer give us a very powerful tool for developing languages provision in new and exciting ways.

Where do we want to be going with languages?

Although the feedback from the 2004 Language Trends survey shows languages positioned in opposition to so-called vocational choices in many schools, in an increasingly global economy, languages must be *par excellence* a practical subject. Projections from regional skills audits show that the need for languages in the workplace is likely to increase at all levels, not just for professional and managerial posts. Language skills are highly relevant, and can enhance employability and job satisfaction across the full range of vocational areas. In many ways we are facing the same challenge of reconceptualising the role of languages in the curriculum as in the early days of comprehensivisation: despite the experience of the National Curriculum and the Graded Objectives movement that preceded it, languages are still seen – not by language teachers but by Headteachers and Curriculum Managers – as an academic subject and not a very fertile area for pupils of all abilities to shine and develop their skills and understanding of the world. How should we be responding to this situation, in the context of the 21st century? Surely not by acquiescing to attitudes which have their genesis in the pre-comprehensive era. But equally, how much should we stress the utilitarian agenda, linking languages to vocational pathways, as opposed to the wider cultural and educational benefits that language learning brings to all pupils? The answer is surely that these viewpoints are not opposed and that cultural and educational development goes hand in hand with employability: languages support pupils' development both **academically** and **vocationally**.

Tomlinson – a lost opportunity?

The Tomlinson proposals, though pushing forward the vocational agenda which appears currently to be damaging languages, in fact offered some very positive opportunities for embedding languages within this. There was a strong emphasis on community languages, as well as the traditional modern foreign languages and a call for the entitlement to study a language to be extended to 19. It was easy to see how languages could fit into core learning and the Open Diploma and there was to be a specialist Diploma in Languages, too. Tomlinson suggested that the languages community might argue for languages as an essential element for those seeking Merit or Distinction in their Diplomas and as a way of adding kudos to vocational options (as in the German system).

Implications of the White Paper

The 14–19 White Paper published in response to the Tomlinson Report has however confirmed that GCSEs and A levels are here to stay for the time being, so it is in these areas that we must continue to secure the future for languages. However it, too, takes up the vocational agenda, providing a challenge to innovate and boost languages within vocational pathways. There is much scope for creativity and new courses for those students for whom GCSE has never proved satisfactory. As the role of the Learning and Skills Councils starts to impact on funding, the views of employers will become more and more crucial. Secretary of State for Education, Ruth Kelly, has said that if employers were to demand a language as an essential part of Leisure and Tourism courses, she would grant their request. That is why it is so important to make the case for languages to our communities, as well as within our schools. Employers are parents and they can be influenced via schools, as well as by many other means (see **www.cilt.org.uk/employment**).

However we must not lose sight of the core of our provision – the half a million students currently taking GCSE languages. We must hold ground for these students as well as finding ways to make the experience more motivating for them. For some, we will be looking at new modes of delivery of the same courses – fast-tracking, content and language integrated learning experiences, Applied GCSE and the offer of Level 1 qualifications.

Why do languages matter so much?

So why is it important for teenagers to learn languages? This is the heart of the matter. Those of us who speak another language understand instinctively the complex range of benefits it has brought us, but how do we explain this to others? And how do we tie in what is good for the individual with what is good for our nation – or indeed humanity as a whole?

Linguists and commentators in the UK and across Europe have taken issue with the 'monolingual perspective' which has been identified as holding back the development of languages in the curriculum. Negative attitudes towards bilingualism are transmitted thoughtlessly in the press ('Britain's worst school has 20 languages') and even among educationalists 'bilingual' is sometimes used as shorthand for 'has difficulty in understanding English'. The climate for languages would be more favourable if we could move on from a monolingual to a multilingual (or, in the terminology of the Council of Europe, a 'plurilingual') perspective, which stresses the value of varying levels of competence in different languages within a European or global context, rather than monolingual citizens of nation states who speak mainly the language of that state plus, if they are among an elite, a 'foreign' language.

How can we explain the vision of 'plurilingual citizens' and make it stick across the range of people we need to influence? Very often we are so busy trying to make a point in one arena that we overlook another area of complexity. Looking at the issues as part of an interrelated framework, such as that developed in one of the Council of Europe's language projects (Facing the future: Language teachers across Europe), might help us to present coherent and consistent messages that reinforce each other, rather than competing for attention and confusing the listener. The human brain is likely to be able to absorb arguments better if they are presented as part of an overarching schema.

The following chart, taken from the Council of Europe publication *Facing the future: Language teachers across Europe*, provides such a schema:

Old mindset	New vision
Focus on the nation state and the national language as a source of identity	Focus on European citizenship and the plurilingual individual
Multilingualism is a problem for society	Multilingualism enriches society
Language teaching assumes learners start from a monolingual base	Language teaching takes into account diverse experiences of languages outside the classroom
Bilingualism and cultural diversity is 'silenced'	Bilingualism and cultural diversity is on show and celebrated
The education of bilingual children is seen as a problem – the focus is on developing the national language	Bilingualism is welcomed – the focus is on developing mother tongue as well as other languages
People who speak other languages are 'foreign'	Speaking another language is normal
It is difficult to learn another language	It is normal to learn another language
Near-native fluency is the ultimate aim	Even lower levels of competence are valued and add to the communicative repertoire of the individual – to be developed throughout life
Language learning is mainly about linguistic objectives. Cultural elements are impoverished, or restricted to 'high culture'. The target-language culture is seen as static	Language learning involves a strong cultural element. Culture is seen as dynamic
Language learning concentrates on one language at once	Language learning makes links between languages and seeks to develop language awareness
Language learning is seen as elitist and languages for all is seen as problematic	Language learning is normal for everyone

(Dupuis, Heyworth, Leban, Szesztay and Tinsley 2003)

If we are to move towards a more positive approach to languages, we must value competence in all languages and their cultures, we must be more tolerant towards partial competences and low-level language skills (near-native speaker fluency is not, after all, the only goal and everyone needs to start somewhere). We must broaden our conception of what language learning is about, to include intercultural skills and knowledge about language in addition to the four skills, so the purposes of language learning are not restricted to a narrow instrumental rationale.

All this valuing does, of course, imply a moral dimension: positive attitudes towards difference acquired through language learning are as important as the ability to transmit information. This is a philosophy in which the idea that some people are not intellectually in a position to benefit from learning languages has no place: if languages are an essential part of education for citizenship within European (or global) society, then they must, of necessity, be for everyone.

Making the case to Heads, Governors and Senior Management

☐ Which arguments are likely to persuade Headteachers, Governors and Senior Management?

☐ What can you do if your school has already made languages optional?

☐ What can you do if languages are still compulsory in your school?

☐ How can you reach your audience?

☐ How can you lock into their current concerns?

☐ How can you rebut negativity about languages?

chapter 1

The main concern of Headteachers and Governors is that pupils should do well. Whether this stems from a positive commitment to the education and development of young people, or more pragmatically a concern with league tables and performance targets is immaterial. It therefore follows that they may be very sympathetic to the idea of greater flexibility in the Key Stage 4 curriculum which will allow pupils to choose courses in which they are most likely to be motivated and to excel. This is where languages loses out through being seen as a difficult subject – particularly for some pupils – and one which pupils are not motivated to choose.

In schools where languages are already strong and producing good results, the challenge will be not to let the new flexibility allow pupils – and staff – to drift away, undermining your school's ability to continue doing well.

In schools where languages bring down overall GCSE scores, the task will be much harder and you will need to suggest measures to improve results (over, say a three-year period), as well as underlining the dangers of allowing languages to fall into even greater decline. Inasmuch as improved results are linked to pupil motivation, you will find some suggestions for improving this in Chapter 4.

In making the case for languages to Headteachers, Governors and Senior Management, you will need to lock into their current concerns and what is driving change within your school, rather than trying to plough a completely separate furrow. Later on in this chapter we give some examples of how to do this. Meanwhile, let's start by rounding up some positive arguments in favour of languages.

Which arguments are likely to persuade Headteachers, Governors and Senior Management?

Depending on the type of school and your knowledge of your Head, you will know which of these arguments are likely to work best.

The internationalist approach

Languages give a school a strong internationalist forward-looking dimension (this can work either for European languages, for example linked to Comenius EU-funding for links and exchanges across the curriculum, or for community languages where a school wishes to make an asset of an ethnically diverse pupil population).

 investigate!

Prestige

Languages give a school status and help stop the drift of middle-class pupils to the independent sector. (Independent schools teach more languages, start them earlier and have higher take-up rates post-16.)

Social inclusion: Class

When languages are optional, it is the middle-class pupils who have been exposed to the benefits of speaking another language who are more likely to continue with them than disadvantaged children with fewer opportunities. This compounds disadvantage and social exclusion.

Social inclusion: Gender

There is also a serious gender gap in languages – around 16% more girls currently sit a GCSE in languages than boys. The pattern of female dominance widens at A level (30% difference), in language degrees (40% difference) and in recruitment to PGCE courses in languages, with the gender gap increasing at each level. Schools where languages are optional are already showing boys dropping out at a higher rate than girls. This, too, is a form of social exclusion.

General education

Languages are an essential part of a broad and balanced curriculum which prepares pupils for life in a globalised society.

Citizenship

Citizenship in Europe should mean having an understanding of another language and culture.

Practice in other countries

UK schools have the shortest period of language provision in Europe. In other countries, languages are compulsory for longer and take up more curriculum time. We also have a lower rate of take-up of the second foreign language.

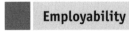
Employability

Employers are increasingly recognising the value of language skills and other skills acquired through language learning such as analytical ability, general communication skills, outward-looking attitudes and intercultural competence. There is a regional dimension to this too, with language skills increasingly being linked to regional economic development. Look at your Regional Language Skills Capacity Audit and use the information there (**www.cilt.org.uk/rln/audits**). Young people without languages are disadvantaged in Europe and in the global economy.

Preparation for life in an internationalised environment

In the world in which these young people will live, literacy and communication skills should include a basic qualification in another language as well as English. Communication is not just about English. In an international world, literacy is being reconceptualised as meaning literacy in more than one language.

Minimum entitlement

The Council of Europe estimates that the minimum number of hours required to reach the 'Threshold' level as an independent user of a language (B1 in the Common European Framework of Reference) is around 350–400 learning hours. Many students will not have received this in three years of secondary education.

National skills shortages

There are not enough young people coming through the system with language degrees. We need to keep up numbers post-14 and encourage more to take languages post-16. We need to secure a supply of high quality language teachers for the future, as well as specialist and non-specialist linguists to support business needs.

What can you do if your school has already made languages optional?

Produce figures for take-up in Year 10 for each year in which languages were not compulsory (if only one year's figures are available, do a quick survey of current Year 9s).

Is take-up increasing or decreasing? In many schools where languages have been made optional, take-up declines year on year unless special measures are taken to guide pupil choices. What will happen to languages if this trend continues? You can argue for:

- restructuring of option blocks so that more pupils are guided into language choices;

- new courses to be included which are likely to appeal to different groups of pupils (one school which offered the Certificate of Business Language Competence as 'Business Language' alongside GCSE found it easily filled both a French and Spanish group. The inclusion of the word 'business' was felt to be a key motivating factor);

- improved careers guidance and advice – is your school using the *Languages Work* materials see page 62 Schools are already starting to report positive results from using these: in one school where languages was an optional subject, a cross-curricular team planned and presented the materials to Year 9 pupils and achieved a 70% take-up in Key Stage 4;

- or you might try to buck the market with an incentive for those that do languages (e.g. access to a ski trip or priority for some other reward) – see Chapter 4 for further ideas.

What are your chances of getting languages reinstated as a compulsory subject? If you make a good enough case, and new courses are successful, you might even manage to do this.

What can you do if languages are still compulsory in your school?

You have the edge – don't lose it. But do you know which of the above arguments were most powerful in clinching compulsory languages? Is the commitment to compulsory languages solid? You need to understand what underlies the commitment, to make sure you deliver to expectations.

You will need to provide positive reinforcement of your Head's decision and evidence of success from the chalkface.

With many schools already having made languages optional, schools where they are still compulsory have an edge when it comes to recruiting the best language teachers. Tell your Head how important it is that your school hangs on to this advantage, both for the morale of current staff and for new recruitment. Teachers do not train to work in Key Stage 3 only and are likely to be put off teaching in a school where there is little stimulating KS4 work. Similarly, if your school is a training school, you will not be able to provide trainees with sufficient experience in Key Stage 4 – teacher-training institutions are already highlighting this as a serious problem.

You can also provide evidence from other schools of the dangers of going down the optional route.

Warn your colleagues of very high student drop-out in schools where languages are offered as a free choice (last year's *Language Trends* survey showed wide fluctuations between schools, but on average 60% of Year 10 students were dropping languages). Schools which made languages optional at the first opportunity have been taken unawares by the extent of drop out, producing some disturbing situations (reported on the Lingu@NET forum):

- one Specialist Technology College reported the complete abandonment of languages in KS4;

- another reported a single group of fifteen in Year 10;

- another school reported that in Year 9 a group of 20 had been removed from languages because of staffing shortages.

Widescale dropping of languages affects talented linguists as well as lower-ability language students and has a knock-on effect on the viability of languages in the sixth form. It also exacerbates gender imbalance in languages.

Demotivation trickles back into Key Stage 3 when languages lose status higher up the school.

Fewer students doing languages means it is more difficult to offer two or more languages.

There may be fluctuations from year to year in the number of students wanting to do a language. This will make planning difficult. Will you be able to guarantee the 'entitlement' to all students if numbers drop? Will your school find itself perhaps relying on non-specialists to teach languages? This will only hasten the decline.

It is very difficult to build up a department once it goes into decline – don't let this happen in your school.

It is clear that it is not acceptable for very large numbers to be opting out in a 14–19 curriculum which is supposed to be 'world class' and develop 'practical skills for life and work'. The Government is committed, through its National Languages Strategy, to increasing numbers studying languages in further and higher education and in work-based training. How can this happen if your Languages Departments are weakened?

How can you reach your audience?

You will need to make your case in a systematic and sustained way, not just on the basis of a snatched conversation in the staff room – though don't be afraid to grasp every opportunity to reinforce your case!

You can reach your target audiences a number of ways:

- Make sure that each Governor and each member of Senior Management receives a copy of the CILT/ALL factsheet for Heads and Governors on languages in the KS4 curriculum. This summarises the statutory situation and the definition of 'entitlement' (see Introduction page 3) and brings together some arguments in favour of languages. You can download a copy from **www.cilt.org.uk/14–19/ governors.pdf.**

- Ask to make a presentation to the Governing Body or Governors' curriculum committee.

- Prepare a paper to hand out, so this can also be circulated to others unable to attend – keep it short and snappy.

- Is there a link Governor for the Languages Department? Is he or she an ally, a potential ally, someone who could do more? Cultivate this person and make sure he or she is well informed and able to speak up for languages. If there is not a Governor linked to the Languages Department, why not ask if one can be designated to fulfil this role? Is there a particular Governor who is likely to be sympathetic to you? Identify your allies and use them.

- Make sure your Senior Management and Governors are well informed about current teaching practice in languages and are able to see the wider educational benefits of learning a language. Invite key individuals into your classes or departmental meetings.

- Make sure languages have a role to play in whole-school events and training days.

- Keep languages visible within the school with displays, literature, on the website and regularly in the school newsletter.

- Show wherever possible how language learning benefits pupils across the curriculum.

How can you lock into their current concerns?

As we have said above, you are more likely to be successful in making the case for languages if you can lock into Headteachers' current concerns and show how languages can support them. Don't approach the issue defensively, from the point of view of the Languages Department, but from a strategic perspective. Offer a solution, not a problem.

The hot topics which concern Heads and Governors will vary according to the changing context and the situation that pertains within the individual school, but for the foreseeable future they are likely to centre on:

- 14–19 reform;
- the new OFSTED framework, *Every child matters* (2005b);
- specific development priorities for your school.

All the above are, of course, related, so the particular priorities of your school are likely to reflect the national picture. Here is one example:

School development priorities

- Introduce/extend vocational learning at Level 1 and 2 in KS4
- Raise GCSE ('Diploma') pass rate
- Establish progression pathways from KS4 to KS5
- Pupil profiling

What you will need to do is to map languages on to your own school's development plan and identify ways in which they can support whole-school objectives. Take a step back and consider, in a very broad-brush (perhaps radical?) way, what these priorities might mean for languages. For example:

Whole School	Languages
• Introduce/extend vocational learning at Level 1 and 2 in KS4	• Introduce vocational and Level 1 language courses
• Raise GCSE ('Diploma') pass rate	• Improve A*–C results in languages
• Establish progression pathways from KS4 to KS5	• Identify talented linguists and an offer enrichment programme
	• Focus on improving take-up in Year 12
	• Offer vocational language courses in the sixth form
• Pupil profiling	• Improve opportunities for students to obtain a qualification in community languages
	• More differentiated pathways in KS4 (fast-tracking, Level 1 courses, etc)
	• Use of the Languages Ladder to accredit single skills (e.g. speaking only)

Don't panic yet! This is not a development plan, just a way of opening up the discussion. You can do it with your department or on the back of an envelope, just as long as you have whole-school priorities in mind when you come to discuss development of the Languages Department with your Head and Senior Management.

Similarly, it is possible to map the contribution of languages against the new inspection criteria in *Every child matters*:

Be healthy	Through topics in the languages scheme of work, e.g. drugs, diet, exercise, healthy lifestyles
	Through learning about lifestyles and attitudes in other cultures
	Sports competitions and exchanges with partner schools in other countries
Stay safe	Topic work on bullying, health and safety issues, etc either in a UK or foreign context
Enjoy and achieve	Cultural activities, visits, etc organised by the Languages Department
	Extra-curricular activities, language evenings, etc, European Day of Languages events E-mail and multilingual clubs
	Provision for and celebration of community languages
	Qualifications and results achieved in languages
Make a positive contribution	Links with other countries, especially third-world countries
	Fundraising and charity events linked to these
	Intercultural learning. Parental and community involvement
	Use of *Languages Work* materials to broaden horizons and deepen understanding of the world of work
	Active involvement of students at all levels (languages are well suited to this)
Achieve economic well-being	Languages as an enhancement to employability, ambition and career prospects
	Work experience with languages; visiting speakers
	Use of *Languages Work*, as above, to develop understanding of languages in working life

Financial literacy: work with Euros and other foreign currencies

Linking with FE and HE. Progression routes with languages

Once again, it is not suggested that you plan to develop all these things at this stage, but you can gather together all the things you already do under these headings and use the framework as justification for more you would like to develop.

Now you will need to have a close look at languages within your school and decide what your priorities are for developing them within these frameworks over the next three to five years. With self-evaluation very much on the agenda in the new OFSTED framework, this is a very worthwhile exercise. As an adjunct to its report on languages in Key Stage 4, OFSTED has published some very useful self-evaluation prompts which will help you structure your thoughts (OFSTED 2005a). Once again, doing this as a department is extremely valuable.

What you should be aiming to produce is a development plan. Here are some of the headings it might cover:

O Current situation of languages in your school (and developing trends over the past three years or so)

O Pupil profiles – which groups do better or worse at languages

O A critique of the current situation and a vision for developing languages within the school – rationales and approach

O Aims and objectives over the next three years (or more)[1]

O How you plan to meet these aims

O Who will need to be involved

O Costs and any other implications

O Measuring progress – evaluation

O Communicating your plan and promoting languages within the school

---

[1] It is not within the scope of this book to provide detailed advice on departmental planning for languages.

By all means spell out the consequences of **not** maintaining a strong enough focus on languages (see page 20), but your message should be positive and forward-looking. Languages will get nowhere if they are seen as a problem with no answers forthcoming. Similarly, if your case is too general, it may not lead to any real action. Be specific. Say what you want to achieve and what you will need to get there.

Tip Are you in touch with your local Specialist Language College? They have a brief to support their community of schools. Is there a new area you would like to develop that they could help you with? For examples of good practice in Specialist Language Colleges, go to **www.cilt.org.uk/languagecolleges** or **www.specialistschools.org.uk.**

Use success stories with languages to show what can be achieved. Examples of successful and dynamic practice with languages in KS4 can be found on-line at:

- **www.cilt.org.uk/eal/winners.htm** – UK winners of the European Award for Languages since 1999;

- **www.dfes.gov.uk/languages/DSP_whatson_secondary.cfm** – case studies of good practice on the DfES website;

- **www.cilt.org.uk/14-19/index.htm** – case studies and a downloadable report of CILT's 2004 conference on languages 14–19;

- **www.cilt.org.uk/languagecolleges/case_studies.htm** – case studies of innovative practice in the Specialist Language Colleges;

- **www.bcsip.org/pathfinder** – inspiration from the work of the Black Country 14–19 Pathfinder.

How can you rebut negativity about languages?

Very often, it's the throw-away line that casts a shadow over languages and those of us who seek to defend them are left searching for words, while non-specialists seem to accept the assertion at face value. Here are the top ten rebuttals to use in such situations.

✦✦ Languages are for the academically able ✦✦

No, languages are not just for the academically able, languages are for all. What better soundbite here than that contained in the title of the Government's National Languages Strategy, *Languages for all, languages for life*? We have to state categorically that there is no pupil who cannot benefit from learning something of a foreign language and its culture. This is reflected in practice in most other countries. In the history of mankind and in the world today, millions of people speak a language they have learnt as a foreign language, not as a mother tongue. They are by no means all academically able; they have not all learned in an 'academic' way. There is an academic approach to learning languages and it is essential that those students who are going to be the specialist linguists of the future (our teachers, translators and academics) are exposed to this type of learning, but not everyone needs to learn languages in this way. Today's world makes communicative demands of all citizens, not just an elite.

SEN pupils benefit from language learning just as much as other pupils, as a host of literature, including a recent EU report (Marsh 2005), makes clear. OFSTED's 2005 report highlights schools with above average numbers of pupils entitled to free school meals, where 90% or more of pupils take a GCSE in a language and achieve results at least as good as in other subjects (OFSTED 2005a). A feature of these schools is leadership committed to preventing languages becoming an elitist subject and to making it a successful experience for pupils of all abilities and all backgrounds.

Even if the notion that languages are for the academically able is not expressed explicitly, it may very well be implicit in people's thinking and that's what needs to be challenged. When people talk about a 'vocational' curriculum or one which students can 'access' more easily, are they really saying that languages are only for the brighter students? We need to make a social inclusion case about the educational benefits of languages for all pupils, as well as the point about languages being a highly practical subject, useful in a wide range of circumstances.

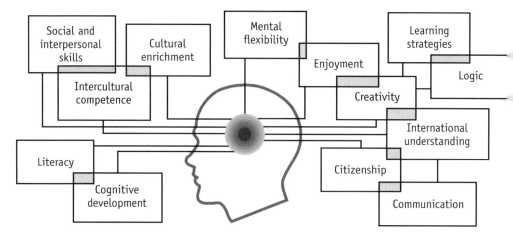

Some educational benefits of language learning

Some children who struggle with literacy in English may have difficulty with the written word in a foreign language – for them the Languages Ladder offers the opportunity to accredit speaking or listening separately. Others may find that their difficulties are linked to English only and may do well in a language with straightforward spelling such as Spanish or German. The experience of learning a foreign language can be highly supportive of literacy in English and boost communicative competence across the board. What we need to ensure is that the type of provision offered to pupils in this category is suited to their needs and does indeed boost their achievement in English and other subjects, rather than being further confirmation of their status as low achievers.

The new more diversified arrangements in KS4 provide just the scope needed to provide differentiated pathways in languages for different types of learners.

66 Languages are irrelevant because everyone speaks English 99

Easy to rebut but actually more complex than at first sight. Not everyone does speak English (only 6% of the world's population speaks it as a first language; about 25% in all, counting second and foreign language speakers). However, it's hard to deny most people's experience of going abroad that English is widely spoken as an international language. This is where we get into the 'yes buts'. Here are some:

- Yes, but that means English-only speakers are limited to what others (who can speak other languages) want to tell us (where they want us to go, what they want us to buy, eat, etc).

- Yes, but in order to build a real relationship with someone (for business or social purposes) you need to meet them half way and know at least something of their language.

- Yes, but this perception is damaging British business – exporters are losing business because of language and cultural barriers. You can buy in English, but you need to sell in the language of the customer. You can also benefit from building relationships by showing you are making the effort. For a full overview of economic arguments, see CILT's 'Talking World Class' leaflet at **www.cilt.org.uk/key/talkingworldclass.pdf**.

- Yes, but they are learning other languages too. We are being left behind as monolinguals in an increasingly multilingual world.

- Yes, but not to each other! We need to understand other cultures and, crucially, understand what it is to be a foreigner.

- Yes, but learning a language has educational not just utilitarian benefits.

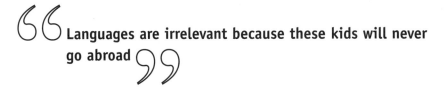

Languages are irrelevant because these kids will never go abroad

A defeatist position which denies the role of education in opening up opportunities. Once again, we need to look here at the educational not just the utilitarian benefits. Learning another language helps one understand better how one's own language works, it provides a reference point of what language is, which is outside the experience of the mother tongue, it teaches intercultural awareness, builds knowledge of other cultures and improves communicative competence across the board.

But, of course, the statement can equally well be rebutted from a utilitarian perspective. Languages are needed at home as well as abroad. Foreign-owned companies investing here want people who can communicate with their head offices and staff. The availability of language skills in a local area is often a major factor in attracting inward investment. We don't need to go abroad to meet speakers of other languages, they are coming to us – as tourists, as business partners, via the Internet and as members of our own communities. Community languages are being valued more and more in public services. International communication is everywhere, it doesn't just come into play through travel abroad.

---

66 Languages aren't worth the effort, because these kids can't even speak English properly! Prioritising English will be what brings real benefits for them 99

What if English is an additional language for some pupils? Have they not already got the benefits of learning another language? And wouldn't greater competence in English serve them better in the long run?

This is a difficult question and the answer will depend on the individual. It may be quite patronising for some pupils to assume that just because they speak, for example, Urdu at home there are not able to learn Spanish at school. Some pupils in this position shine in foreign languages precisely because they have had a rich linguistic experience at home.

Other more recent arrivals or those who have not had a solid linguistic experience in the past may indeed struggle with English, but find that in the foreign language classroom they are on a level playing field, precisely because there is less emphasis on English, and again, they can do well.

Others would benefit most from support with their home language as well as English and the recognition that achieving a GCSE or other qualification in their home language might bring. In these cases, the chance to do Panjabi, for example, as an alternative to French in curriculum time would be of huge benefit.

 Languages don't produce good enough results

This issue is also dealt with in Chapter 4, since this may be an issue for pupils as well as Heads, Senior Management and Governors. The question is, is this true in your school? How do language results compare to other subject areas and to national figures? If they compare well, there is no case to answer – simply make sure everyone is aware of the facts. If they compare badly, you will need to analyse the reasons why and include proposals for improving them in your development plan. There is no need now to hang on desperately to GCSE for all – the new arrangements allow you to be creative and experiment with new models, though make sure you are prepared to subject them to rigorous evaluation.

GCSE language courses are not suitable for some students

This is self-evidently true – at both extremes of achievement, just as it is for other subjects. Between 39% and 46% of entrants nationally fail to achieve a Higher Level grade in languages – a similar proportion to other subjects. However, fewer than 1.5% were ungraded in languages in 2004, compared with 3.6% in Art. The point is not to let people confuse the characteristics of a particular course with the value of the subject. GCSE will probably remain the mainstay for most students, but now is the time to innovate and introduce alternative models tailored to the needs of different groups of students.

66 There's no point in forcing kids to study languages 99

This is, in fact, the basis of current Government policy, though some would say that if they are forced to study Maths and English (not to mention subjects like Citizenship). then why not foreign languages, too? Successful language learning depends on motivation, so we take the point that unless students think it is worthwhile continuing with a language then the benefits will be reduced. However we are shirking our responsibilities unless we ensure they have adequate information on which to base their decisions and are given a strong steer in the right direction. Too many children give up languages through ignorance of the world about them and that's no basis on which to make judgements. Too many adults regret not having got further with their language learning when they were young. Use of the *Languages Work* materials can prove very valuable here. See Chapter 4 for ideas on how to get the best out of these materials and other suggestions for making the subject more appealing to learners.

66 They don't learn enough for it to be worthwhile 99

What is 'enough'? We are talking about Level 2 qualifications here, not degree level. If your Head believes that Level 2 is not enough, then logically he or she should surely be encouraging all students to take a language at AS and A2? It is not justifiable to make this statement about languages and not about other subjects and cast languages as 'only' of utilitarian value and 'only' if a high degree of fluency can be achieved. In business, on holiday and in a whole range of social situations, a little language can make a lot of difference. It is unrealistic to expect students to emerge as fluent native-speaker equivalents in the relatively short curriculum time available, but we can provide them with a good basis to build on in later life when the need arises. Whether they want to spend a year abroad as part of their degree, open a car-hire firm on the Costa del Sol, or need to learn a new language for their work, having a recognised level of competence on which to build will make all the difference. It's not just words and grammar they are learning, they are experiencing what Eric Hawkins calls 'an apprenticeship in language learning', i.e. learning how to learn a language, strategies for communicating with speakers of other languages, as well as a degree of intercultural awareness. In today's multicultural world, everyone needs this, not just those who are going to use their language skills directly.

---

66 The curriculum is overloaded – pupils will do better if allowed to concentrate on fewer subjects 99

There is a valid case here – with so many peripheral subjects (Citizenship and now Enterprise Education coming on stream) and the need to give sufficient time to the core subjects, pupils can be doing fourteen or fifteen subjects and this puts a huge strain on their ability to organise themselves, let alone absorb the lessons from each. Languages have got a key card to play here, in that the content is not fixed and links well with areas of content across the curriculum (ICT, Music and Drama, Literature, History and Geography, as well as Citizenship and Enterprise Education). So the answer is to show how languages can contribute to some (not all!) of these content areas and so enrich the curriculum as a whole. In the next chapter we will discuss links to literacy, citizenship and enterprise education. If you can show that pupils will be getting a rich educational experience – and developing a skill at the same time – you will be in a strong position.

---

66 Languages are hard 99

This notion needs to be unpicked a little. Do we mean that pupils perceive languages as hard? Is this to do with classroom practice, or with the structure of the exam system? Whichever way, there are things we can do to alter their perceptions and help them take pride in their achievements. See Chapter 4 for further discussion of this. And if pupils do find a subject hard, does it automatically mean that they don't want to do it? You may need to talk to pupils directly, or even better, give them a questionnaire, to get to the bottom of some of these issues in your school. Research shows that the identification of language learning as something that is hard to do can be a self-fulfilling prophecy (Jones and Jones 2001), so we definitely need to address this perception at its root.

By 'hard', do we mean perhaps that we think languages produce lower grades for the same effort, i.e. that they don't produce good enough exam scores? This may be a preoccupation for Heads and Governors, and you will need to test this proposition in your school – see 'GCSE language courses are not suitable for some students' above and the section on pupil preoccupations page 70. Is there evidence that pupils are working harder than for other subjects and getting lower grades? Do they really do as much revision in languages as for other subjects? And, given the extent of work they need to do for say Art, is it really the amount of work which is a demotivating factor?

Perhaps what is meant is just that languages are intrinsically hard. But, just as with other subjects, this depends on what level we are working at in relation to the abilities of our students and how well we help them to achieve appropriate goals. When Heads and other decision-makers refer to languages as 'hard', it may be that they are taking themselves back to their own experiences of language learning, which they may perceive as having been unsuccessful or irrelevant to them in later life. Make sure they are aware of current practice. Languages are different from other subject areas in that progression is not related to content. Pupils are asked to acquire and then synthesise a range of different skills – pronunciation, vocabulary, the relationship between writing and sound, sentence structure, cultural conventions – and think of something relevant and meaningful to say at the same time! Communicative competence is not something that teenagers necessarily have in large amounts in any language, but it doesn't mean that they don't need the practice.

Non-specialists – such as colleagues in Senior Management – are often very bad at giving the right level of credit for achievement in language learning. Either they think progress is poor, and therefore not worthwhile, or they can see the whole process as overwhelmingly complex and too much for pupils to master. We should recognise that progress is not linear and that different types of learning are involved at different stages. And we must communicate the fact that this is what gives language learning a unique contribution to make in the curriculum. And at age 14 plus, students can start to draw on strategies such as analogy, knowledge about the world and the way people interact in a more sophisticated way, and so can get more out of their language learning. Some pupils may surprise us with their ability to imitate, or to pick up some aspects of language intuitively. Other subjects are hard, too, but languages are different and they deserve special consideration for that reason. So, yes, some aspects of language learning may be hard, but that's no reason for not doing it.

Key documents

- ALL/CILT factsheet for Heads: **www.cilt.org.uk/14–19/heads.htm**

- QCA guidance: *Modern Languages in the KS4 curriculum*: **www.qca.org.uk/ 13680.html**

- OFSTED guidance and self evaluation tool: **www.ofsted.gov.uk/publications/ index.cfm?fuseaction=pubs.summary&id=3933**

- The Government's National Languages Strategy, *Languages for all: Languages for life*: **www.dfes.gov.uk/languagesstrategy**

key points	• **Offer solutions, not problems for your Headteacher and Governors**
	• **Lock into their concerns, don't plough a separate furrow**
	• **Show how languages support whole-school objectives**
	• **Rebut negative thinking about languages**

How to persuade and involve other departments within the school

- ☐ Does your school have a languages policy?

- ☐ How do you raise the profile of your department and change the attitudes of Senior Management and other staff?

- ☐ Could you do more to recognise pupil achievement?

- ☐ What can be gained from working more closely with other departments?

- ☐ How can you maximise the opportunities provided by international links and exchanges?

chapter 2

Language learning is about communication, opening horizons and giving us a door to open onto on a new world. Increasingly, school communities are becoming more multicultural and multilingual. New immigrants, enhanced language competencies in local communities and pupils from other countries add to the richness of the school environment, but how easy it is, in these days of points, targets and league tables, to get trapped within the confines of the languages classroom and forget the wider community just outside the doors, whether that's the immediate circle of colleagues and other staff within your school, the family and friends of your pupils or the more extensive local community. Yet in the new landscape for languages in schools, these are the people that we're going to need to win over if language learning is to continue in meaningful and inclusive ways.

The obvious place to begin is close to home, in your own school and with your own colleagues.

First and foremost, as we have pointed out in Chapter 1, it is Headteachers, Senior Management and Governors who need to be convinced about the importance of languages, not just of learning languages and not just those languages which are taught and learnt in your school, but of **languages per se**.

Does your school have a languages policy?

A useful starting point for opening broad discussions might be to focus on a whole-school language policy. This may well be a first step towards making an opening for languages – or a bigger space for the subject – in a school where language teaching is struggling to maintain its position. To argue for the importance of languages, especially the home languages of pupils within the school, raises significant issues about equality and inclusion which will make a good springboard for later discussions about the place of foreign languages in the curriculum.

This short publication is not the place to raise the many complex issues which surround the needs of pupils whose access to the curriculum is through a different language. It is, however, worth bearing in mind that these may be powerful arguments in the creation of a whole-school language policy.

On a more practical level, points you could raise with Senior Management and Governors are:

• Would it be good practice to have a written statement of general principles taking account of the linguistic needs of all pupils and parents? (This may well exist already in your school.)

(It could help your case to refer to the link between cultural and linguistic respect and discipline and the promotion of good behaviour.)

- Should home languages or mother tongues of pupils and teachers be more visible around the school?

(It should be possible to work with other colleagues – from English, EAL, SEN – on such an initiative.)

- Would it be helpful to conduct a languages audit among both staff and pupils?

- Is language capability valued? And if so, how?

- There may also be opportunities to mention languages in other school-wide policies. The list below contains some suggestions, although it is by no means exhaustive.

School policies which would benefit from the inclusion of languages

Statutory	Recommended	Additional (good practice)	Other
• Careers and work-related learning • Home/school agreement • Race relations • School journey • Staff development	• Equal opportunities • Exam policy • Support of NQTs	• Ethnic-minority achievement • Independent study • Work experience	• Languages policy

A strong lead at Senior-Management level can help to change staff attitudes generally and this should be another goal. The attitude of other members of staff to languages is vital if languages are going to be accepted as a valuable and desirable part of the curriculum for all. How do your colleagues who teach other subjects behave when they walk into a languages lesson and are confronted with another language? How do teachers of other subjects deal with foreign words in their own classrooms? It will depend to a great extent on personality and foreign language capability, of course, but their reaction may well help to set the tone for the whole school when it comes to attitudes to language learning. Colleagues are often very reticent to talk about their own capability (or what they often perceive as lack of capability) in languages, yet many will have partial knowledge of another language, some will be proficient and yet others may be bilingual. Do you know the language capabilities of your colleagues teaching other subjects? Has anyone ever tried to find out? Could you create opportunities for staff to become involved in language learning or to pass on their own language skills to pupils (try Speed Languages below)? The European Day of Languages is an annual event which provides excellent opportunities for whole-school language activities which include staff. Possible activities and resources are presented on the CILT website (**www.cilt.org.uk/edl**) and you can add your own events to the European database on the Council of Europe website (**www.ecml.at/edl**). Stressing the benefits of plurilingualism and recognising that partial competence in other languages is both advantageous and desirable will provide a good base upon which to build your case for the place of foreign languages in the curriculum.

Case study	The European Day of Languages at Worle Community School

To celebrate the European Day of Languages in 2004, Worle Community School, a Media Arts College in Weston Super Mare, put on two activities which enabled a whole-school approach to raising awareness of other languages and cultures.

Speed Languages

They came up with the wonderful idea of 'Speed Languages'. This gave pupils and teachers the chance to learn a little of as many different languages as possible in their lunch break. Fourteen teachers (from across all curriculum subjects) and one pupil taught a real A–Z of languages in a list that started with Afrikaans and ended with Zulu (and, yes, both of these really were included!).

Zulu

Speed Languages, which is based on speed dating, gives each participant the opportunity to have a three-minute introduction to a language before a whistle signals them to move on to the next language.

European Treasure Hunt

Ten teachers each represented a different European country. During the day, pupils had to find out from each teacher information about 'their' country, for example its flag and how to say 'hello' in the language. As they progressed, pupils also collected a French word each time to complete a mystery sentence.

How do you raise the profile of your department and change the attitudes of Senior Management and other staff?

Let others see your work – it sounds simple but it doesn't always happen. There are many ways that you can showcase language learning, all of which may help to raise awareness of your subject within the school and promote language learning.

- Report regularly on initiatives and achievements within the school community to pupils, parents, staff, the Headteacher, Governors and the wider community (see the Elliot School newsletter case study, page 53).

- Invite others – pupils and staff (including Heads of Year and tutors) – to come along to pupils' presentations.

- Make information available to staff who play a key role at options time – Heads of Year and careers staff.

- At options time, promote the links between languages and other curriculum subjects.

- Organise group visits to films, plays and other events, especially those in the new language – and invite staff, from both languages and other subjects, as well as pupils.

- Display pupils' work around the school, not just in the languages classrooms.

When the profile of language learning is raised, pupils gain a sense of pride in their achievements and this should improve motivation.

The Wilson Stuart School, Erdington, Birmingham

The Wilson Stuart School, Erdington, Birmingham, is an all-age school for children with physical disabilities. It shares a campus and a languages teacher with the Priestley Smith School for blind and visually impaired pupils. In both schools the Headteachers fully support the learning of a foreign language throughout KS3 and KS4. In the past ten years, only three pupils have been withdrawn despite their numerous disabilities. French is taught to the greatest possible number of pupils and there is a strong emphasis in the school on integrating the foreign language teaching into whole-school activities. Many of the things they do are simple and do not require much in the way of additional resources, but taken together they build strong support for French within the school. Pupils see French all around the school: all rooms are posters support topic work being done in other subjects. A star system rewards pupils for using a French word anywhere on campus. Activities include a French Day when all school staff, from Headteacher to dinner ladies, join together to give one day a year a French flavour, with the school canteen being turned into a French café. French also has its place in some of the daily school activities and extends to other curriculum areas. For example, some of the pupils require regular intensive physiotherapy and they count their exercise routines in French.

Although French is the only language in the curriculum, language awareness is encouraged around the school and pupils' home languages are often used in language-awareness activities. Recently, the French teacher brought back a number of menus from Croatian restaurants which were all in four different languages. She devised a competition based on family resemblances of words and this led to comparing words in the pupils' own languages:

> *Thus we learned that* ananas *was used in Somali, Urdu and Pashto and that* chemise *was the word for a top in Urdu.*

It will help you personally in the promotion of your subject to keep up to date with what's happening in language learning both regionally and nationally. This will be of benefit in discussions in staff and parent meetings. It will give you credibility with your Headteacher and with your colleagues and be evidence of your own professional commitment. Both CILT, the National Centre for Languages and the Association for Language Learning have membership schemes through which teachers can keep up with the latest developments in language policy and current practice. You can find out more on the ALL website (**www.all-languages.org.uk**) and on the CILT website (**www.cilt.org.uk**).

Could you do more to recognise pupil achievement?

Recognise your pupils' achievements by:

- awarding prizes for academic excellence, outstanding effort or good progress;
- publicising their success in community newspapers and other media – for example high exam results, trips and work experience abroad, gifted-and-talented programmes;
- entering them into competitions and cultural events and recognising their participation and achievement.

Young Language Leaders

Some Specialist Language Colleges have been piloting this scheme, which you might be able to join, adopt or adapt to recognise achievement in foreign language learning. Selected pupils become Language Leaders and use their language skills actively within the school community. This might be by:

☐ visiting local primary schools to support the language learning of younger pupils;

☐ participating in school events, for example by providing foreign language content for school concerts;

☐ supporting pupils in lower years taking part in international projects, perhaps by writing letters to partners;

☐ producing materials for other pupils;

☐ creating presentations for the school website.

Case study | Little Lever School Specialist Language College

In Little Lever School Specialist Language College, Bolton, Year 8 pupils have prepared and taught Saturday morning sessions to Year 6 pupils. The eight Young Language Leaders attended all of the twelve sessions. They were supported by a teacher at first, but then progressed to taking the sessions themselves. They kept a diary of their activities and made a PowerPoint presentation for the school website. Year 8 pupils wrote poems, which were translated into French, Gaelic, German, Portuguese, Spanish and Urdu by staff in the school and published in book form with translations. Year 9 pupils taught French to Year 6 pupils during summer-school activities. Year 8 and 9 pupils are planning to teach Year 6 pupils in Saturday-morning language workshops. Year 10 ran a lunchtime club for language learners and pupils in Year 9 and Year 10 have taught English in France and during the German exchange. Former pupils have taught during intensive language days.

Year 9 pupils were involved in an international awards activity involving 'hands of friendship'. They organised the collection of hundreds of 'hands' with foreign language greetings written by younger pupils. They arranged for the collection, helped with writing and posting of the 'hands' to Belarus, Mexico, Russia, Germany, Spain, Japan and France. They are hoping to receive 'hands' from these countries for display.

What can be gained from working more closely with other departments?

Internationalism and cross-curricular links

The positive and varied benefits of language learning are not the major focus of this publication, but before going on to discuss the opportunities for cross-subject links, we should pause to consider the contribution that language learning has to make to more generic parts of the curriculum – literacy, citizenship and intercultural understanding, personal development and education.

Where languages are taught in challenging and difficult circumstances, for example, a common experience seems to be that language learning increases self-esteem and raises general levels of literacy. The new Key Stage 2 Framework for Languages relates closely to the National Literacy Strategy and at KS3 many parallels are now drawn between learning English and learning a foreign language. It is important to stress the relationships between literacy, competence in the mother tongue and foreign language learning, especially to colleagues in other subjects for whom these advantages of foreign language learning will not always be apparent.

Learning a foreign language helps develop:

- an awareness of basic grammar – parts of speech, sentence construction, grammatical terms;
- the notion of different tenses;
- a sense of the history of language and the links between different languages;
- reading and listening for gist;
- the ability to guess at meaning;
- strategies for memorising and spelling;
- dictionary use;
- confidence in speaking;
- communication with others in pair, group and whole-class work;
- reading of different kinds of text or texts, presented in different ways, using a range of media;
- an understanding of register;
- an awareness of the complexity of all languages;
- the notion that language is not one fixed system.

For further reading on this topic see:

- 'Common approaches to literacy and language' (Rose 2002)
- *Literacy, Numeracy, Citizenship and MFL* (Cruickshank 2003)
- Key Stage 3 National Strategy: *Framework for teaching Modern Foreign Languages – Years 7, 8 and 9, Foreword* (DfES 2003)
- Young Pathfinder 9: *The literacy link* (Cheater and Farren 2001)

Schools are now beginning to investigate the possibility of cross-curricular links which involve languages, often (in response to the Internationalism agenda) in combination with a link with a school abroad. Some have even gone a step further and introduced an element of content and language integrated learning (often referred by its acronym CLIL, the term used for any subject that is taught through the medium of a language other than the mother tongue, e.g. History through

German, Geography through French, Citizenship through Spanish) into their programmes. For more details on CLIL see **www.cilt.org.uk/clip/faqs.htm**. Specialist Language Colleges are at the forefront of such work, although it is by no means limited to these specialist schools. The Government's new focus on internationalism will help to take forward initiatives such as these and to recognise the contribution that language learning can make to other subjects. Indeed, as one of the benefits of languages is that it is content free, it is hard to think of a single curriculum area where languages could not play a part.

Working with other staff on cross-curricular or cross-school activities raises their awareness too, helping them to see that languages can add value to many subject areas. At the most obvious level, you might think about:

- sports activities; *ski trip?*
- one-off project work with another subject;
- special events;
- drama productions in the foreign language;
- languages and music or arts projects;
- working with the school kitchen on food/languages events;
- Food Technology and languages;
- digital video projects involving other staff and departments.

Cross-subject initiatives such as Citizenship and Enterprise Education are also good vehicles for languages to work with other subjects, as well as being fertile ground for language learning generally. CILT, the National Centre for Languages has produced an information sheet which suggests how language teaching can support the objectives of Enterprise Education and this is full of useful ideas (**www.cilt.org.uk/14-19/enterprise_ed.pdf**).

The cultural, and more especially intercultural, aspects of language learning contribute to the Citizenship agenda and here, again, there are good opportunities for cross-curricular work – understanding what makes other nationalities behave as they do, recognising that our own behaviour is not the norm but part of the infinite variety of human behaviour, influenced by the culture into which we are born. The publication *700 reasons for studying languages* also has excellent interactive Web pages at **www.lang.ltsn.ac.uk/700reasons/700reasons.aspx**. Here you can search on a number of key words to find reasons for learning languages associated with your search words. A search on 'citizenship' brings up sixteen reasons, as well as other links to follow and references to further reading.

Here's just one example:

> *Citizenship education calls for the teaching of values, understanding and skills as well as knowledge about life in other communities to help pupils develop a respect for cultural diversity. Language teachers have particular experiences to draw on (many will have spent a year abroad) which give them a vital role to play in the teaching of citizenship in schools. Language teachers have much more personal experiences of the issues that lie at the heart of citizenship education.*

The DfES Standards website also has a leaflet to download which maps the areas where the MFL and Citizenship programmes are compatible, see **www.standards.dfes.gov.uk/pdf/secondaryschemes/citsubject_mfl.pdf**.

How can you maximise the opportunities provided by international links and exchanges?

Exchanges and visits have always been a part of the activity of most Languages Departments in the UK. However a number of developments have recently had a negative impact on exchanges and visits, including high insurance premiums and police checks on parents involved in exchanges. There is some evidence that the number of overseas visits by pupils is falling (*Language Trends 2004* survey). The 'marketing' potential of trips abroad is big and in some schools the most popular subjects at option time can be those with the best trips on offer! If you are involved in exchanges and visits abroad, then exploit them for all they're worth both in and out of school (see also Chapter 3). There may also be potential to piggy back on trips offered by other departments by organising short language courses, tasters, self-access courses or language-learning advice for staff and pupils involved, for example Italian for the skiing trip, German for the history trip to Berlin, or you could include language work when abroad.

Pupils in or returning from a country where the languages you teach in your department are spoken can also help to raise the profile of languages by sharing their experiences with other pupils, either through your newsletter or by using on-line environments. Some schools are now beginning to experiment with weblogs and a Languages Department in Scotland, at Musselbrugh Grammar School, has been blazing a trail in this respect.

Case study | Musselburgh Grammar School

Musselburgh Grammar School (a comprehensive on the outskirts of Edinburgh, with over 20% of pupils on free school meals) has an on-line international project which brings together Languages, Citizenship and ICT. The project brings international relations and languages to life through a range of technologies, including weblogs. Recently, they have also been the first school in Europe to podcast, allowing subscribers to download audio files automatically. These and other resources are regularly accessed on-line by staff and pupils to help with teaching, homework and revision.

International links, trips abroad and the opportunity for virtual exchanges have had a positive impact on the take-up of languages in terms of students taking a second language in S3 and continuing in S4 and S5 (S stands for secondary and the number for the year of secondary education). Those involved have a more realistic idea of foreign cultures and a clearer understanding of the similarities between young people across the world.

The project won a European Award for Languages in 2005 and the judges said:

> The involvement of Modern Languages in Citizenship work is seen as crucial for improving take-up of languages in the school. It enables pupils who believe that they may not be likely to travel abroad or meet foreigners in their local area to gain a wider understanding of what links people from different countries and why it is important to be able to communicate.

It's well worth a visit to the website at **www.mgsonline.org.uk** to get a flavour of all the different kinds of work and projects in which the school is involved.

Visitors from another country will have an impact both in school and in the wider school community through family hosting arrangements, outings, and special occasions in school to welcome and say goodbye to visitors. School trips can also help to involve parents and families in languages and cultural experiences (see Chapter 3).

Plan of action

Finally, while this may all sound a bit overwhelming, remember that you don't have to do it all and you don't have to do it at once. Promotion should be part of your departmental development plan and would provide a good focus for departmental meetings. Discussing among colleagues how you might go about raising the stakes for languages would be an excellent first step and could lead to a simple plan of action for the first year (or specified period). A written document provides all staff with an agreed agenda, a point of reference and a basis for review at the end of a trial period. It provides Senior Management and Governors with evidence of the seriousness of your intent and your commitment to take positive action in what could be difficult times for your subject.

key points	• Schools and Languages Departments need to gain and maintain support for languages
	• Within the school, it is important to share information (including careers information), acknowledge students' achievements, arrange exchanges and visits, and acknowledge the diversity of the school's languages and cultures.
	• Within the community, a school can establish links and publicise its language activities.
	• A plan of action can help a school to promote languages effectively.

How to persuade and involve parents and the wider community

☐ How good is your communication with parents?

☐ Are there opportunities for you to work more closely with other providers in your local area?

☐ Is there a way you can link in to local businesses, local government or the local media?

chapter 3

How good is your communication with parents?

If colleagues in your school are the first to feel the impact of the language-learning experiences going on in your classroom, the next should be the parents and wider social circles of your pupils. The National Languages Strategy for England (DfES 2002b) talks about the need to change our culture:

> *If we are to contribute to this wider social change and to persuade young people and those who influence them most closely that foreign languages are important and the effort to learn them worthwhile, then we need to involve parents, carers, family and friends.*

While some parents will have informed and positive views about many aspects of learning languages, many may well have no real knowledge or experience of language learning (beyond, unfortunately, often negative school experiences themselves) and will see this as a subject area where they have little to contribute. Yet we know that the majority of adults in the UK believe that it is important to learn languages (*Eurobarometer 54*, Education and Culture Directorate General 2001), so we can have some confidence that any promotional work we do won't fall on deaf ears. In our experience, parents of young children – and not only those who live in leafy suburbs (see the case study on the ALLEGRO project below) – usually want their children to learn languages; they see capability in foreign languages as an attractive attribute for their children, one which equates with educational and social success. It is interesting, therefore, that some of this parental support for language learning seems to be lost by the time children reach their mid-teens, with certain parents bemoaning the fact that their children are obliged to continue with language learning at this stage. We need to give them the tools and knowledge to be able to help to encourage and support their children through the difficult teenage language-learning years. There are many different ways of involving parents in languages. Here are just a few ideas that some language departments have used:

- Invite parents to come in during the first term in Year 7. Let them see a typical language lesson, take part in taster sessions themselves and see their child perform in the foreign language. Let them share their child's success in this language-learning phase and give them ideas about how they might support their child's progress (see *Bringing it home: How parents can support children's language learning,* Farren and Smith 2003).
- Develop a clear, concise written statement for parents and pupils that includes the reasons for learning languages and the objectives of the courses in your department.

- Invite parents to take part in whole-school language activities, perhaps on the European Day of Languages.
- Use pupils to 'teach' parents in after-school and evening clubs, or as part of homework tasks.
- Have a parents' information evening for KS3 – explain policy, the KS3 Framework, invite an external speaker, build relationships with parents across this key stage. If you're worried about getting parents along to this kind of activity, involve the pupils – parents like to see their children 'in action' and children will usually pile on the pressure for Mum or Dad to attend.
- Collaborate with a local AE centre or with those who teach languages in the community in your own institution to offer some family language-learning opportunities (see the case study on family learning below).
- Use the parents'/carers' questionnaire in *Languages Work* to raise awareness of the value of learning languages (*Teachers Booklet:* 19).

The Languages Ladder, introduced in September 2005, should provide opportunities to celebrate steps in language-learning success with parents and families. It will also provide accreditation for initiatives like family learning.

In communities where children come from a variety of linguistic backgrounds and where many parents speak other languages, the kinds of whole-school activities discussed in the Case Studies in Chapter 2 (e.g. Speed Languages) could well involve parents as a resource.

Case study | Spanish Mums' Night

The Spanish after-school club at Halsnead Community Primary School, Knowsley, put on a Spanish mums' night where children who had been learning Spanish for a term invited their mums to come along to get a taste of the action. The children taught them how to count to ten (using the **www.literacycentre.net** website), followed by a game of bingo; they played 'What's my line?' and had to identify the professions in Spanish; they used an interactive whiteboard to teach their mums the names of animals and then pairs (mother and child) took part in a competition based on the activity. At the end of the evening, everyone went home with stickers and an enormous sense of satisfaction. In the words of Roy Topping, the teacher who worked with the group:

The night provided the children with an audience for their work and an opportunity to use their Spanish beyond the normal classroom setting. The thing I found especially pleasing was to see the children teaching their mothers, consolidating their knowledge with their mums clearly enjoying the experience.

A full account of this initiative may be found in *MAPE Focus on MFL: ICT supporting Modern Foreign Language teaching and learning in primary school* (Wake 2003: 15).

Virtual links may also provide ways of keeping parents in touch with what's happening in languages. The languages pages on your school website, for example, could give information about what pupils learn from day to day, with ideas about how pupils can develop their knowledge outside the classroom and how parents can contribute to this. International links, visits and exchanges will provide plenty of opportunities, from real encounters with visiting pupils from other countries, through interesting items in the languages newsletter, to the possibilities that ICT provides to keep in touch with pupils abroad. The weblogs idea in Chapter 2 helps keeps groups on trips abroad in touch with other pupils, teachers and parents at home.

Case study | Elliot School newsletter

The Specialist Schools and Academies Trust (SSAT) currently has on its website examples of school newsletters featuring languages. The SSAT is keen to encourage Specialist Language Colleges to 'inform parents, students and the public about how much you value the teaching and learning of languages and your cross-curricular and international links'.

At the time of writing, the termly newsletter of Elliott School, a Specialist Language College in south west London, was available on the SSAT website. Articles in the Elliot School newsletter included news on a successful funding application to the British Council to take eleven students on a two-week residential course in the summer holiday to Beijing, a report on a Year 8 visit to the Goethe-Institut accompanied by a pupil's report in German, where to find good GCSE revision sites, a Citizenship/Spanish visit to Spain.

Examples of newsletters are to be found regularly on the SSAT website at **www.schoolsnetwork.org.uk.**

Are there opportunities for you to work more closely with other providers in your local area?

And it's not just parents who need to be involved, but brothers and sisters and wider families. The link with siblings in primary is going to be of particular importance and involving them in activities in your school could establish solid ground upon which to build in future (see Young Pathfinder 13: *Mind the gap: Improving transition between Key Stage 2 and 3,* Bevis and Gregory 2005).

Your local Comenius Centre should be a good source of information and support if you would like to take some of these ideas further, especially if you're looking for speakers or contacts. For details of the Comenius Centre in your region, see **www.cilt.org.uk/comenius.**

And so the community grows, beyond your colleagues, beyond parents and families of your pupils and into your local area. Here, again, is another rich source of potential champions of languages and allies in helping you convince your pupils that languages matter. What do you know about your local community in terms of languages?

For example, in education:
- Which languages are taught at your local university? Does the Languages Department work with local schools? Some interesting collaborative work is being done in a number of areas: this ranges from staff and students from universities making one-off visits to schools, to larger-scale mentoring and 'buddy' programmes. The website of the Subject Centre for Languages Linguistics and Area Studies (**www.lang.ltsn.ac.uk**) is a good starting point. In the *Languages Box* Web pages (link from home page) there is advice on how to arrange a visit to your school from a local higher-education institution. As you will see from the case study below, such collaboration can be a real two-way exercise, with schools having a resource to offer to universities, as well as the other way around.
- How is lifelong language learning organised in your community? There might even be adult classes in your own school that you could make links with or you may have a large adult-education college in your area with large numbers of adult learners attending classes. What is the potential here for links and collaborative activities that will enthuse both groups of learners and help you to raise the profile of language learning?

- What is happening in your local, and especially feeder, primary schools?
- How well prepared are you for the intake of learners who will have an experience of language learning in primary (which may be very soon for some secondary schools)?

Case study	Moseley School

Every year in June, Year 9 pupils take part in an event organised by PGCE course tutors at Birmingham University. The pupils teach their home language to MFL ITT lecturers and their postgraduate students. In 2005, the languages offered by pupils were Bosnian, Somali, Arabic and Panjabi; they spend time in school preparing resources to teach their language. They also receive some coaching on language-teaching methodology. The event raises the self-esteem of the pupils involved. They realise that by being bilingual they possess a much sought-after skill and become aware of the difficulty others find in learning their language. It also gives the university students the chance to feel again what it's like to be a beginner in a new language.

Is there a way you can link in to local businesses, local government or the local media?

Languages in the world of work

- Do local businesses and services use languages?
- How?
- Do they employ native speakers or foreign language speakers?
- Would they be possible contacts for your school?
- What are local needs in terms of languages?

Language skills capacity audits have been carried out in most of the English regions and these could be useful background reading. The research plots provision for language learning in all sectors of education and also surveys language services and the availability of native speakers in each region. For further details see **www.cilt.org.uk/rln/audits.htm**.

- Could you give regular information to employers and invite them to school events?
- Could you invite speakers to talk to student groups on a language-related topic?
- Do you exploit the resources available?

Each of the English regions has a Regional Languages Network and a gateway to the websites of the various networks can be found at **www.cilt.org.uk/rln**. You should find them a useful tool for finding out more about how businesses are using languages in your region. Some of the websites have pages directly related to business and education partnerships, for example the South West Regional Languages Network (**www.rln-southwest.com/EducationProviders/default.aspx**).

One initiative supported by the Regional Languages Networks is the Business Language Champions scheme, where successful individual business people from the region work with education providers to highlight the increasing need for employees with language skills and to provide opportunities for practical experience of using languages at work. See **www.rln-southwest.com/blc/default.aspx**.

Case study | Students get a taste of business life

South Dartmoor Community College had a valuable insight into the importance of learning foreign languages when Business Language Champion Geraldine Bedford of gro-group international visited the school to show students how the company is looking to languages to maintain its export success and expand into new markets.

The company and the school are both based in Ashburton, Devon and there are plans for students to visit the company and to look at work-experience opportunities. The partnership has had some great ideas for projects with languages, making leaflets in French, advertisements and letters to distributors, letting the students gain real hands-on experience.

Geraldine Bedford explained her reason for getting involved in the initiative:

> We are very keen to encourage students to continue with their foreign language learning, as they will be key to the success of South West

businesses in the future. Without them, companies like ours will not have a pool of talent to draw from. Most companies have a website these days, which means that they are an international business from the word go. Having access to language skills is important, as this can prove to be the difference between making or losing a sale.

Sarah McDermott, Head of Modern Languages at South Dartmoor Community College described the value that the students got from the presentation:

Taking part in the Business Language Champions project and working with gro-group international has meant that students at South Dartmoor Community College have been able to see how foreign language skills are an essential business tool.

This opportunity has provided them with a unique insight into how they could use foreign languages in a South West company in their future career and is the key to encouraging them to continue studying languages. Students are able to see the relevance of languages outside the classroom, which is vital.

With gro-group as our Business Language Champion we have been able to bridge the gap between foreign language learning in the classroom and how languages are used every day in the world of business. Having a local South West champion based in the same town has given the students a unique learning opportunity, which we hope to build on in the future.

Some schools have had disappointing experiences when trying to make links with the world of business. There is a potential culture clash and both sides need to be aware of where the other is coming from. Links with business work best where education and business can see clearly – and make explicit – the advantage to them in any relationship. It's a two-way process.

Opportunities for languages in local government

- Is there twinning activity?
- What is the international policy?
- Could you invite speakers to talk to student groups on a language-related topic?
- Could you exploit the resources available?

Working with the local media

- Could you publish articles and photographs in the local newspapers?
- Or publicise information on school visits, exchanges and language events in local libraries?

There may be opportunities for you to take languages outside your institution. Perhaps you could visit a nursery, school or old people's home and show them what you do in languages, or involve them in some taster sessions. Activities such as these help make foreign languages a reality in the community and the people upon whom they have an impact may well be parents, grandparents or family members of your pupils. They also provide good 'human-interest' stories which local media may pick up on.

Case study | Nottingham Trent University and the Vale Centre

Although this example refers to work done by a university, it could be adapted by a school as a community or citizenship project.

As part of the 'Allegro' project, a European Commission-funded initiative, the Languages Department at Nottingham Trent University worked with the Vale Centre, a community centre in one of the most disadvantaged and challenging inner-city areas in Nottingham, to put on languages drop-in sessions for mothers and pre-school children. Mothers were taught simple games, rhymes and songs to do with their children. The foreign language varied from session to session and food and drinks were provided for those who took part. Some young mothers visiting the centre for other activities but who did not wish to participate were also encouraged to watch. Feedback from staff in the centre, the languages teachers and the women themselves was very positive: they were learning positive parenting skills (playing with, singing with and teaching their children), the fact that they were doing this in a foreign language made it a 'special' activity. Mothers having this experience may well go on to be more supportive of their child's foreign language learning later in life.

The ALLEGRO project won a European Award for Languages in 2005. For further details about the project, see **http://allegro.acs.si**.

Case study | Campion School and St John's Secure Unit, Tiffield

Campion School, a Specialist Language College in Northamptonshire, works with a local unit which provides secure care for young people from 11–16 years of age. Foreign Language Assistants from the school visit the secure unit throughout the year to teach the young people who find themselves there something of the language and culture of the countries from which the Foreign Language Assistants come. The pupils enjoy finding out about other countries from teachers who are quite close to them in age. The experience raises their self-esteem and helps broaden their horizons.

Although it is not possible in such a project to involve the pupils at Campion School directly, the fact that the school itself works in such an innovative way to support what are often 'forgotten' children in their local community, brings success and recognition to both the Languages Department and to the whole school community. The project won a European Award for Languages in 2005.

Members of the community who are speakers of the language being learned may appreciate opportunities to be involved in creative ways, such as assisting with drama presentations, music, cookery and art, and sharing their experiences.

Once more, we are talking not just about making languages successful in your school, but about taking positive steps towards making that vital culture shift that will help us move from a monolingual to a multilingual society.

Case study | Joint adventures in Barcelona

The Black Country Pathfinder and Creative Partnerships team worked collaboratively to fund Year 9 pupils from Deansfield High School in Wolverhampton to visit Barcelona for three days in July 2005. The project links academic and vocational learning with the world of work.

The project started in September 2004. From the beginning, pupils kept journals and diaries as a way of recording the activities they undertook, as well as their thoughts and feelings. Pupils visited Birmingham Airport and were given a guided tour to see the facilities and hear first-hand from staff how they utilise languages within their professional context. This was a great way for pupils to prepare for their departure for Barcelona, as well as contextualise the Spanish they were learning at school.

Pupils also visited the University of Wolverhampton on two occasions, gaining a glimpse of life as a university student and receiving a lecture in Spanish from a member of the School of Humanities, Languages and Social Sciences lecturing team.

Throughout the activities pupils were positive and enthusiastic, looking forward to each different aspect of the project and taking ownership by planning their trip to Barcelona.

Their feedback indicates that they now view languages as an essential vocational skill and have been very pleased with their new business language curriculum. The partnership with Creative Partnerships has meant that the language-focused project was embedded across other curriculum areas in the school. As a direct result of this project, recruitment into language courses at the school is up by 40% this year.

key points	• **Don't underestimate the need for parents to understand your subject and what you do – it could be vital in the future**
	• **Look for every opportunity you can to tell the wider community about your successes**
	• **Find ways to get involved with your local community**
	• **There is strength in partnerships with other organisations**

Pupil power

☐ Do teenagers really hate languages?

☐ What sort of motivation are we talking about?

☐ How can I make the most of the *Languages Work* materials?

☐ What can we learn from the world of marketing?

☐ How should we respond when pupils ask, 'What's the point?'?

chapter 4

Do teenagers really hate languages?

The idea that some pupils believe languages are boring and irrelevant is at the heart of the new reforms. Stephen Twigg, the former schools minister, is on record as saying that there is no point in trying to 'force feed reluctant teenagers to study languages' and this observation reflects that fact that languages is a subject, perhaps more than any other, which requires motivation to learn.

We all know that there are pupils whose motivation leaves much to be desired (and not just in languages!), but where schools have removed the compulsion to study languages, pupils have been opting out in very high numbers – up to 90% in some cases. Is it fair to attribute this to dislike or distaste for the subject in all cases?

Surveys of pupil attitudes have painted a mixed picture, but not one of wholesale dislike and rejection of the subject. The *Invisible child* research in Barking and Dagenham, which sought the views of Year 9 children of average ability, found that 75% thought it was important to learn a language and that pupils who appeared unmotivated were not necessarily negatively disposed towards learning a language (Lee, Buckland and Shaw 1998).

Barry Jones's study of boys' performance in languages surveyed 1,266 boys and girls in Years 9 and 11 and found only about 20% saying languages were 'not important' and well over a third saying that languages were 'very important' or 'important' (Jones and Jones 2001). The biggest group, however – nearly a half – thought they were 'fairly important'.

What emerges is not a picture of active dislike, but one in which pupils are mildly positive towards languages. The issue we are facing is that this lukewarm attitude is not enough to drive pupils towards choosing languages when they are faced with a range of other options. The *Invisible child* research found that pupils rated languages second from bottom out of seven subjects.

What sort of motivation are we talking about?

With languages a compulsory subject from 11–16 for the past decade, teachers have not needed to focus a great deal on the extrinsic motivation of pupils, but have rather sought to motivate them intrinsically through their teaching approaches. The authors of the *Invisible child* explicitly counselled against too much emphasis on 'utilitarian' arguments about the usefulness of languages, which they regarded as 'unlikely to be sustained for all pupils'. The *Languages Work* package of materials is specifically designed to redress this balance and boost pupils' extrinsic motivation.

Dornyei's motivational framework, which Gary Chambers outlines in *Reflections on motivation* is a useful tool for thinking about different levels of motivation:

- The language level – perceived usefulness and desire to acquire the particular language being learnt. Contact with the target-language community and its culture.
- The learner level – students' self-perception, confidence, degree of anxiety, etc.
- The learning situation level – the course, content and materials, the teacher, the learning group.

(Chambers 2001: 7)

It is far beyond the scope of this book to go into detail on any of these variables; we include them to assist the reader in locating what follows within a wider context where teaching approaches, course content and pedagogical concerns are rightly given due importance.

Languages Work

'We base our choices mainly on the quality of the lessons. We need to know more about the opportunities' (Year 9 pupil)

The *Languages Work* materials were published in September 2004 with a focus on raising awareness about the usefulness of languages in working life. They fit, therefore, very much into Dornyei's 'language level' of learner motivation. However, the research and development for the materials uncovered barriers at learner level which hold them back from making a positive choice about languages:

> *I'm so dumb I could never learn a language if I tried* (low self-esteem as a language learner)

> *By the time I'm rich enough to travel abroad, I'll be able to afford a translator* (ignorance and bravado born of lack of opportunity – does it also belie an underlying fear that choosing a language will involve expensive school trips which they will not be able to afford?)

> *We're not sure what we're going to do and it might not involve languages* (uncertainty – and possible low aspiration – regarding the future)

> *I'm going to work in the West Midlands* (misconception that languages are needed only if you are going to work abroad)

The *Languages Work* materials have been developed to help overcome these barriers, within the Careers Education Guidance Framework of 2003. They therefore help young people:

- to understand themselves and the influences on them;
- to know how to seek further information and research opportunities;
- to be able to make secure decisions about their future.

They also take into account the 'learning-context' level in that they are intended to be integrated into careers guidance and other subject areas (e.g. Citizenship, Enterprise Education – see page 45) throughout the school and not be the unique responsibility of the Languages Department.

Feedback from schools which have used the *Languages Work* materials has been extremely positive and pupils have responded well. In one school there was an immediate spectacular leap in take-up for AS – from four to twenty for French and from one to eleven for German! Evaluation of the *Languages Work* materials is ongoing at time of writing but it appears that, probably through lack of time, the full potential of the products has not yet been explored and they could be more widely used in schools, particularly by careers teachers and form tutors.

How can I make the most of the *Languages Work* materials?

It is likely that you will already have seen the *Languages Work* materials, and have a copy of the *Activity folder* (CILT 2004) in your school, but you may not yet have found time to exploit their full potential. Here is a checklist of action points for making the most of *Languages Work*, in particular in Key Stage 3:

✓ The posters are displayed in prominent positions throughout the school (not just within languages classrooms – the messages they convey are meant for other teachers, Governors and parents, as well as pupils).

✓ Use of the questionnaire for parents and carers (see *Teacher's booklet* page 19). Schools which have used this at the time when option choices are being made report good impact. The questionnaire can be printed out from the CD-ROM and a copy given to every child to take home.

✓ A copy of the *Languages Work handbook* for your careers guidance staff

(Knowles and Luddy 2004). This is a vital reference tool for them. Are they aware that this exists? You should also have a copy easily accessible for pupils to consult.

 Have all your Year 9s (at least) received a copy of the 'Mind your language' factsheet? Printing out a black and white copy from the website or CD-ROM and photocopying it is probably the easiest way of getting the numbers required. You can also order multiple copies (up to 40) from CILT to have available at parents information evenings, etc.

 Have you used any of the video clips on the CD-ROM? These are a good way of drawing in staff from other departments, since they make an interesting resource to spark off discussion and reflection on a whole range of related topics. For example, careers teachers could use the clip of the BMW apprentices who are learning German, or the chef working in Barcelona, and follow up with the lesson suggestion for KS3 on page 13 of the *Teacher's booklet*. This helps get pupils thinking about themselves and start to make the link between languages and what they might be doing in the future. Equally, the clip 'What do I get from Europe?' – a comedy sketch – could be used by a form tutor or PSHE teacher looking at Citizenship, Europe or the international economy. Bringing these resources to their attention is a good hook for starting the process of embedding the *Languages Work* materials throughout the school. Ideally, the longer-term aim should be for planned input in each of the key stages and sustained, coherent messages being given about languages throughout the school.

If you have ideas and suggestions about using the *Languages Work* materials, please let CILT know, so we can pass them on to others and feed them into future development. For further information about *Languages Work*, and to download free materials, go to **www.languageswork.org.uk**.

What can we learn from the world of marketing?

The new arrangements for Key Stage 4 mean that students are more than ever being cast as consumers in a market-driven curriculum and, like it or not, we will have to make sure our subject is able to compete. Perhaps we should take the marketing analogy one step further in order to help us to think creatively about how we should respond. There are tools we can borrow from marketing which can help us to make a better case for languages and improve our 'product' at the same time.

Tip
You could, for example, use the framework of a SWOT analysis to stimulate departmental discussion. Here is a hypothetical example:

Strengths	Weaknesses
• Good results from top set: high proportion of As and Bs • Exchanges with France and Spain • Annual languages and drama event • Regular CPD for staff	• Overall, results in languages lower than in rest of school, especially for middle and bottom sets • Key member of staff has just left • High proportion of reluctant learners, especially boys

Opportunities	Threats
• Introduce new courses as alternatives to GCSE • Deepen link with Drama • Create link with ICT • Lunchtime/after-school revision classes to boost results	• Languages will become the preserve of higher-ability pupils • Languages Department will shrink and be weakened • Languages will become marginalised by move towards more vocational courses

Marketing is aimed at existing customers, too – it helps them feel they have made the right 'purchasing' decision and reinforces brand loyalty. So these techniques may be useful to you whether or not you need to fight for student numbers in your school – they should help to increase motivation across the board.

Try thinking about languages in your school in terms of the five Ps of marketing:

P RODUCT Is our product well-suited to students' needs? How can we use the new flexibility to tailor the languages offer to different groups of students? (See Appendix page 75 for a list of alternative qualifications.) Experience in the Black Country found that enjoyment levels and motivation to learn were raised when the Certificate in Business Language Competence was introduced (Sargeant and Harnisch 2005).

PRICE

Is the price right? In other words, are students getting value for money? Will the grade they eventually get at GCSE or in some other form of certification, merit the effort expended? It is our job to convince students that it will – once again by making sure the product is suited to their needs and is of high quality.

PLACE

Is the Languages Department a pleasant place to be? Is it welcoming and does it provide an environment that is conducive to learning? Obviously there are constraints in terms of buildings, furnishing and equipment (though this is no reason not to argue for better facilities), but there is no excuse for tattered three year-old posters flapping off the wall.

PEOPLE

We know that for languages, more than any other subject, the teacher's role is crucial. This was a key finding of Barry Jones's research into boys' under-performance in languages and he, in fact, suggests strategies for reducing the centrality of the teacher and giving pupils more control over their learning. Nonetheless, you can make the point forcefully when arguing for training budgets and planning professional development at whole-school level, that in languages more than any other subject teachers need to communicate enthusiasm and bring the subject to life with anecdotes and real-life examples. Their access to ongoing professional development – subject-specific and in the target-language country – is critical.

PROMOTION

What messages do pupils receive about languages? Who do they receive them from? As the rest of this book has made clear, it is important that the Languages Department seeks support from colleagues in marketing its subject. We know that the importance pupils attribute to different subjects is determined as much by implicit messages (e.g. how much curriculum time is given to a subject) as by explicit ones (Harland et al 2002). Are there mixed messages within the school about the importance of languages? How are bilingual pupils treated, for example? Are their language skills recognised and valued? It is not convincing for a teenager to be told that languages are important if practice within the school contradicts this.

At a more basic level of promotion, how do you describe the language courses in the school's handbook for option choices? Or on the school website? Are there ways in which you can improve on either the text or the presentation? How about some attractive visuals, or quotes from 'celebrity linguists' (see below)?

Tip If you find it useful to look at your offer in this way, you could use 'the five Ps' as a basis for further departmental discussion – or even as a way of setting out your case to Senior Management.

Promotional techniques

However much we may dislike the idea of treating pupils as 'customers' this is the situation we find ourselves in. So, having analysed our situation according to marketing principles, what techniques can we bring in from the world of advertising that can help us promote our subject? (Why, after all, should the devil have all the best tunes?)

Incentives □ Otherwise known as shameless bribery – can be anything from a tin of biscuits from Brittany to a week's trip to Barcelona (though the latter would obviously not come free!). Feedback from pupils as part of the *Languages Work* development work showed that trying foreign foods came out tops in terms of what pupils liked about their language lessons. There is scope to do more eating in language lessons! On another tack, what about a 'free gift' for every student starting a KS4 language course? One school which had used stickers and bookmarks in the past found 'scoobies' went down very well!

Peer marketing □ Have you got an enthusiastic group of Year 11s or sixth-formers? Use them to get the message across. They will be able to deal honestly with some of the concerns your Year 9s might have about taking a language for GCSE (or other course), e.g. the amount of work, how hard it was to get a good grade, how to revise best, etc.

Satisfied customers □ Testimonials or case studies of former students from your school who have gone on to use languages or study for a degree with languages. Where they went for their year abroad and what they are doing now. Even better – invite them to come in and talk to your current students face to face. Experience in Wales, where a foreign language has never been compulsory in KS4, shows that real-life examples of **local** young people are what is most convincing.

Celebrity endorsement □ Don't underestimate the power of 'the Beckham effect' (which manifested itself as a huge leap in OU recruitment to Spanish courses when he first signed up with Real Madrid). Use the concerns of the pop media to fight your own cause – make links with what pupils see and hear daily and bring out the language dimension. CILT has a list of celebrity linguists, with quotes in some cases, at **www.cilt.org.uk/edl/linguists** – keep a look out for new ones likely to appeal to your pupils.

Ask an expert □ Bring in outside speakers to say what you could say perfectly well – but it carries so much more weight coming from an outsider. This is the equivalent of the scientist in the white coat saying how good the washing power is. It works!

Relationship marketing □ You make the product 'fit' so well with their aspirations and image of who your customers want to be that it becomes a 'must-have'. What 'brand image' will sustain your pupils' through the more tedious parts of their course? Global citizen? International business success? Gap-year explorer? Young European fashionista? (And does the term 'Modern Foreign Language' really do it for pupils? Doesn't it immediately make the subject sound old-fashioned and bookish? Why not just 'languages'?)

Try if you'll like it □ What about a 'taster' KS4 lesson, or a first go with an exercise from a GCSE paper. A good morale-booster.

NEW! □ Don't underestimate the novelty value of a new course or a new language (say Chinese or Japanese). Like any new product, it has to be thought through and done well. But keeping your customers is about continuous innovation – and the new arrangements for KS4 offer an exciting opportunity to diversify your offer.

External pressure □ Strong advocacy from those in authority. Get the Senior-Management team, the careers service, form tutors and parents all saying the same thing and watch your figures increase!

Buy one, get one free □ Team up with another curriculum area (Geography, Art, History, ICT) to make some sort of joint offer. This could be a cross-curricular project, a school trip linking the two departments, or even an experiment with content and language integrated learning (see **www.cilt.org.uk/clip**).

Special events □ Think particularly about the European Day of Languages – 26 September each year. Many schools have already absorbed this date as a regular fixture in the calendar and there is a wealth of good practice and creative ideas to draw on. See **www.cilt.org.uk/edl**. Other days when you might find an 'excuse' to organise a special event around languages are:

1st Thursday in March	2nd Monday in March	21 March	27 March
World Book Day	Commonwealth Day	World Poetry Day	World Theatre Day

9 May	May	21 May	21 September
Europe Day	Adult Learners' Week	World Day for Cultural Diversity (UNESCO)	International Day of Peace

26 September	October	October	November
European Day of Languages	Black History Month	Family Learning Week	International Education Week

November	16 November	18 December	
Enterprise Week	International Day for Tolerance	International Migrants Day	

How should we respond when pupils ask, 'What's the point?'?

The *Languages Work* package provides material for addressing three major misconceptions:

- everyone speaks English;
- you need to be fluent;
- languages have no value for me.

It is not the intention of this book to rehearse answers to these questions; they are well covered in the factsheets 'Mind your language' (for younger pupils) and 'Work talk' (for Key Stage 4 and above).

There are other questions which teachers find themselves asked every day and unless they have given some consideration to their replies, they may be unwittingly demotivating pupils.

What's the point of studying languages? It is very difficult to give a succinct answer to this, not just because languages are important for so many different reasons, but because learning about why languages are important in a wider context is closely connected to children's developing maturity and their understanding of the world about them. But a long drawn-out answer about a privileged route to intercultural awareness will not convince. Teenagers will expect – and will be happy with – a sound bite or 'elevator pitch' they can easily repeat to their friends or parents at a later stage. Here are some suggestions – it's worth thinking them through to consider which would go down best with your pupils and how to bring them to life with examples they can relate to. This can be done as a department, possibly.

- Because they're there. (They're a fact of life, there are 6,000 languages in the world and they all work differently. Don't you think it's a good idea to learn how at least one other language works and be able to say something in at least one language that's not English?)

- Because everyone needs to have a basic knowledge of another language, like Science or Maths. (Tricky ground, but only the most alert teenager will spot that languages are not actually designated as a basic skill in this country – though you can point to the fact that they are in most other European countries.)

- Because languages are a practical skill that is becoming more and more useful – think how international everything is becoming now. (Add a nice local or personal example if you can – or perhaps refer to the BMW apprentices on the *Languages Work* video clip.)

- Because they are a very good thing to have on your CV – employers will be impressed and you'll have more opportunities to do interesting things in your work – such as travel abroad or work with foreign clients. (Again, give a good example here, such as the motor mechanic who got to work for Formula 1 because he spoke Italian.)

- Because if you've learnt one language it is much easier to learn another – and you might have to do that in future for all sorts of reasons.

- Because it helps us to understand people from different cultures – not everyone sees things the same as us and it's easy to misinterpret behaviour we don't understand. (A good example here would be the continental habit of kissing.)

- Because you can have more fun when you travel abroad if you can communicate with local people. (Say something about the particular language they are studying.)

- Because you'll cut off opportunities if you give up languages too soon. Let yourself get to a good level with a qualification before you decide languages are not for you.

I'm no good at languages

This is Dornyei's learner level – anxiety about performance. Low self-esteem may not be linked to languages. What do you say? An honest answer is always best. 'I think you could quite easily get a C' could be an immense boost to some pupils. Or, 'Are there some bits you find particularly hard? What are they?' What if you know they have no chance of getting even a C? This is where the new arrangements allow you to innovate and put on courses where all students can feel they are successful. As the Languages Ladder comes on stream it will be extremely useful in this respect, too.

I can get a better grade with another subject

There is no evidence nationally that GCSE students are getting better marks in other subjects than in languages. The proportion of A*–Cs was slightly below average for French compared to other subjects in 2004, but well above for Spanish. It is impossible to tell from the national figures whether the different proportions of A*–C grades for different subjects reflect the ability of students taking them or the effort expended by them, but it is unlikely to reflect a greater intrinsic difficulty – though there are concerns about this at AS level. You will need to look at your own results to answer this question fairly. Are your language GCSE results lower on average than other subjects in your school? If so, your pupils are making an informed market decision in dropping languages and you will have to do something about this before you can expect more pupils to opt for them. Another way of looking at it, from the students' point of view, is that they may be able to get the same grade for less effort with another subject. Here peers' views and the school grapevine come strongly into play. Taking into account curriculum time and revision time across the two years, do you think that it is fair? Most Languages Departments would probably say their results suffer because students spend too little time working on their own, not that students are working twice as hard to achieve the same results. Be honest and change what you can.

I won't need languages for my career

The way you reply to this can lead down a number of paths and it is worth thinking through which one is likely to be most effective with the particular pupil involved. You can follow the utilitarian argument: 'Well, you'd be surprised how much languages are needed in all sorts of jobs nowadays …', or you can question their assumption that they already have their life worked out and know it won't involve languages: 'Well, you're going to have lots of choices in the future and if you don't do a language you'll be cutting off some of those choices …'. For either of these two replies, the next step is *Languages Work* – both the website and the *Handbook* provide a host of examples of languages in use in different careers. And it's not just careers that use languages every day that need to be stressed, but the unexpected delight in being able to communicate when the situation presents itself. The alternative pathway is to make the educational case. No, you might not need a language for your career, but you will have reached a certain level of education which includes a language, and that will say something about you and who you are in the future. How many of today's adults regret not having had the opportunity to continue studying a language at school?

Why didn't you do something more exciting with your languages than become a teacher, Miss?

Teachers need to be good role models for language learners – as many, of course, are. But the excitement they need to communicate about their subject is all too easily lost in the hurly burly of school life. In answering this question, there are more don'ts than do's: Don't say the rather negative 'I couldn't think of anything else to do', or 'I didn't want to be a translator'. Think of what made languages special for you and the things you have experienced as a speaker of another language that you would never have done otherwise. 'I went trekking in Guatemala', or 'I got asked to help interpret at a football match' – then say why you became a teacher. Let them see that languages are part of your life outside your career, as well as integral to it. It is well worth giving some thought to this question in advance so that you are prepared. Use the opportunity, too, to say what other opportunities there are besides teaching.

Why are we learning this? I'll never need to know it

Who has not heard – and been irritated by – this remark? Yet it is a sign that pupils are questioning and demanding to be active participants in their learning. Again, it needs some thought in advance. A too honest answer – 'You can never tell exactly what you will need –' may actually be demotivating. Pupils may feel they have no priorities to hold on to. A quick reply, 'Because you'll need it for the exam,' may be convincing in the short term but is ultimately limiting. A better reply might be, 'Well I didn't think it was very important either, but last year it did come up in the exam'. You will need to judge whether the pupil is ready for a more philosophical answer about how language learning works: 'It's like a snowball, you need a certain amount to start with, then more will stick to it'. Probably the best reply would be, 'Well, what do you think you will need to say?' You can give them time to come back to you, if you like, and then be sure you work their answer into your scheme of work. At Gordano School, near Bristol, they have based their whole departmental philosophy on teaching students what they want to say – with some spectacular results. They have found that this is in fact the best way to prepare for the GCSE exam. See **www.cilt. org.uk/eal/2004/winners04/winner_talk.htm** for further details.

I want to do something more practical

Isn't it strange how some people can't understand that languages is a practical subject? Is this a problem of ingrained attitudes, or received wisdom, that needs to be overturned, or is it to do with the way you teach languages in your school? Do you provide enough opportunities to use the language, as well as learn it? Use opportunities such as Enterprise Days to build in some fun and active use of the language. Don't have them, in the words of Eric Hawkins, forever doing exercises on the edge without ever getting into the water and trying to swim.

Departmental discussion

Look at each of the above quotes in turn and decide as a department how best to respond. Do they point to any other actions that you could take as a department to help make languages stronger in your school?

key points

- With languages now an entitlement we need to give more attention to promoting extrinsic motivation than in the past

- Marketing techniques can provide inspiration for 'selling' languages to pupils

- Pupils respond to snappy, well-grounded sound bites with local examples they can relate to

Appendix: List of alternative qualifications to GCSE

Board	Qualification	Matches KS4 Programme of Study	Entry	1	2	3
ABC	Certificate in Practical Languages	Allowable alternative	✓	✓	✓	✗
AQA	Entry Level Certificate	Yes, NC levels 1–3	✓	✗	✗	✗
AQA	AVCE Language Units	No	✗	✗	✓	✗
City & Guilds	Vocational Languages	Allowable alternative	✗	✓	✓	✓
Edexcel	Entry Level Certificate	Yes, NC levels 1–3	✓	✗	✗	✗
Edexcel	VCE Applied Language Options	No	✗	✗	✓	✓
Institute of Linguists	Certificate in Bilingual Skills	No	✗	✗	✗	✓
NCFE	Certificate in Foreign Language	Allowable alternative	✗	✓	✓	✗
OCR	Entry Level Certificate	Yes, NC levels 1–3	✓	✗	✗	✗
OCR	Certificate in Business Language Competence	Allowable alternative	✓	✓	✓	✓
OCR	VCE Language Units	No	✗	✗	✓	✗
OCR	NVQ Language Units	Allowable alternative	✗	✓	✓	✓
WJEC	Entry Level Certificate	Yes, NC levels 1–3	✓	✗	✗	✗

Please note that while these details were correct at the time of writing, they are subject to change. See **www.openquals.org.uk** for current details of accredited qualifications.

References

Bevis, R. and Gregory, A. (2005) Young Pathfinder 13: *Mind the gap: Improving transition between Key Stage 2 and 3*. CILT, the National Centre for Languages.

Boaks, P. (1998) 'Languages in school'. In: *Where are we going with languages?*. Nuffield Languages Inquiry.

Chambers, G. (ed) (2001) Reflections on Practice 6: *Reflections on motivation*. CILT.

Cheater, C. and Farren, A. (2001) Young Pathfinder 9: *The literacy link*. CILT.

CILT (2004) *Languages Work Activity Folder for Schools*. CILT, the National Centre for Languages.

CILT/ALL/ISMLA (2004) *Language Trends 2004* (www.cilt.org.uk/keytrends2004. htm). CILT, the National Centre for Languages.

CILT/QCA (2000) *Modern Foreign Languages and Literacy at Key Stages 2 and 3* (**www.cilt.org.uk/literacy/report.pdf**). CILT/QCA.

Council of Europe (1996) *Modern Languages: Learning, teaching, assessment. A Common European Framework of reference*. Cambridge University Press.

Cruickshank, A. (2003) *Literacy, Numeracy, Citizenship and MFL*. Pearson.

DfES (2002a) *Extending opportunities, raising standards* Green Paper. DfES.

DfES (2002b) National Languages Strategy: *Languages for all, languages for life*. DfES.

DfES (2003) Key Stage 3 National Strategy: *Framework for teaching Modern Foreign Languages – Years 7, 8 and 9*. DfES.

DfES (2005) *14–19 Education and Skills White Paper*. DfES.

Dupuis, V., Heyworth, F., Leban, K., Szasztay, M. and Tinsley, T. (2003) *Facing the future: Language educators across Europe*. Strasbourg: Council of Europe Publishing.

Education and Culture Directorate General (2001) *Eurobarometer 54 survey: Europeans and languages* (http://europa.eu.int/comm/education/policies/lang/languages/barolang_en.pdf). Brussels: Education and Culture Directorate General.

Farren, A. and Smith, R. (2003) *Bringing it home: How parents can support children's language learning*. CILT.

Harland, J. et al (2002) *Is the curriculum working? The Key Stage 3 phase of the Northern Ireland Curriculum Cohort Study*. NFER.

Harrison, P. (2004) *Modern Foreign Languages at KS4 in the North East Region*. Regional Language Network North East.

Jones, B. and Jones, G. et al (2001) *Boys' performance in modern languages: Listening to learners*. CILT.

Knowles, J. and Luddy, D. (2004) *Languages Work Handbook for languages and careers*. CILT, the National Centre for Languages.

Lee, J., Buckland, D. and Shaw, G. (1998). *The invisible child*. CILT.

Marsh, D. (2005) *Insights and innovation: Special education needs in Europe – the teaching and learning of languages*. Finland: University of Jyväskylä.

Moys, A. (1996) 'The challenges of secondary education'. In: Hawkins, E. (ed) *Thirty years of language teaching*. CILT.

OFSTED (2005a) *'You don't know at the time how useful they'll be …': Implementing Modern Foreign Languages entitlement in Key Stage 4* (www.ofsted.gov.uk/publications/index.cfm?fuseaction=pubs.summary&id=3933). OFSTED.

OFSTED (2005b) *Every child matters: The framework for the inspection of children's services*. OFSTED.

QCA (2004) *Modern foreign languages in the KS4 curriculum*. QCA.

Rose, M. (2002) 'Common approaches to literacy and language'. *Literacy Today,* 33.

Sargeant, H. and Harnisch, H. (2005) *Vocational progression routes in MFL and their contribution to motivating take-up post-14.* University of Wolverhampton.

Wake, B. (ed) (2003) *MAPE focus on MFL: ICT supporting Modern Foreign Language teaching and learning in primary school.* Newman College with MAPE/NAACE.

DH

418.
007
12
PAR